BX2003 .Q47 1982

Institute for Worship Studies - Florida

The Gospel in the Church

Property of
INSTITUTE FOR WORSHIP STUDIES
Orange Park, Florida

THE GOSPEL IN THE CHURCH

A Catechetical Commentary
on the Lectionary

CYCLE C: THE CREED

Quentin Quesnell

CROSSROAD · NEW YORK

1982

The Crossroad Publishing Company
575 Lexington Avenue, New York, NY 10022

Copyright © 1982 by Quentin Quesnell
All rights reserved. No part of this book may be reproduced, stored in a retrieval system, or transmitted, in any form or by any means, electronic, mechanical, photocopying, recording, or otherwise, without the written permission of The Crossroad Publishing Company.

Printed in the United States of America

Library of Congress Cataloging in Publication Data

Quesnell, Quentin.
  The Gospel in the church.

  Based on the General catechetical directory.
  Includes index.
  Contents: —Cycle C. The Creed.
    1. Catholic Church. Lectionary. 2. Bible—Homiletical use. 3. Bible—Commentaries.
4. Catholic Church—Catechisms and creeds—English.
I. Catholic Church. Congregatio pro Clericis.
Directorium catechisticum generale. II. Title.
BX2003.Q47 1982   230'.2   82-9951
ISBN 0-82450-0454-2 (v. 3)   AACR2
ISBN 0-8245-0476-3 (pbk. : v. 3)

Unless otherwise indicated, English Scripture quotations are taken from the Revised Standard Version of the Bible, copyrighted 1946, 1952, © 1971, 1973. Quoted with the permission of the National Council of the Churches of Christ in the U.S.A., Division of Education and Ministry.

Contents

Foreword by Rembert G. Weakland, O.S.B.   ix

General Introduction   1

Introduction to Cycle C: The Creed   7

The Nicene Creed   9

THE SEASON OF ADVENT
"He will come."

    Luke and the Prophets
    First Sunday   12
    Second Sunday   15
    Third Sunday   17
    Fourth Sunday   20

THE SEASON OF CHRISTMAS
"For us and for our salvation
he came down from heaven."

    Luke 1–2, the Infancy Narrative
    Christmas Midnight   22
    Christmas Dawn   24
    Christmas Day   26
    Holy Family   28
    Solemnity of Mary, Mother of God   31

Second Sunday after Christmas 34
Epiphany 37

Luke 3, the Baptism of Jesus
Baptism of the Lord 39

THE SEASON OF THE YEAR
(Sundays in Ordinary Time before Lent)

1 Corinthians 12–15, on the works of the Spirit (Luke 1-5)
Second Sunday 42
Third Sunday 45
Fourth Sunday 49
Fifth Sunday 51

Luke 6, the Great Sermon (1 Corinthians, contd.)
Sixth Sunday 53
Seventh Sunday 56
Eighth Sunday 59

THE SEASON OF LENT
"For our sake he was crucified."

Luke 22–23, the Passion, Death, and Burial
First Sunday 62
Second Sunday 65
Third Sunday 67
Fourth Sunday 70
Fifth Sunday 73
Passion (Palm) Sunday 76
Holy Thursday 79
Good Friday 82

THE SEASON OF EASTER
"He rose again in fulfilment of the Scriptures."

John, Acts, and Revelation, on the risen life (Luke 24)
Easter Vigil 85
Easter Day 85
Second Sunday 88
Third Sunday 91
Fourth Sunday 96

Fifth Sunday 99
Sixth Sunday 102
Ascension 106
Seventh Sunday 110
Pentecost Sunday 113
Trinity Sunday 115

THE SEASON OF THE YEAR
(Sundays in Ordinary Time after Easter)

Galatians and Luke 7–9, on faith, love, law, and the mystery of Christ and the Church
Ninth Sunday 119
Tenth Sunday 122
Eleventh Sunday 125
Twelfth Sunday 128
Thirteenth Sunday 130
Fourteenth Sunday 133

Colossians and Luke 10–11, on growing up in Christ
Fifteenth Sunday 137
Sixteenth Sunday 140
Seventeenth Sunday 143

Luke 12–14 and Hebrews 11–12, on Christian faith and salvation
Eighteenth Sunday 147
Nineteenth Sunday 149
Twentieth Sunday 152
Twenty-first Sunday 155
Twenty-second Sunday 158
Twenty-third Sunday 160

The Pastoral Epistles and Luke 15–18, on the Church in the world
Twenty-fourth Sunday 164
Twenty-fifth Sunday 167
Twenty-sixth Sunday 170
Twenty-seventh Sunday 173
Twenty-eighth Sunday 176

Twenty-ninth Sunday   179
Thirtieth Sunday   183

1 Thessalonians and Luke 19–21, on redemption and the last things
Thirty-first Sunday   185
Thirty-second Sunday   188
Thirty-third Sunday   191

Luke 23, on the kingship of Christ
Thirty-fourth Sunday   195

Index to the Articles of the Creed   198

Foreword

There have been no end of attempts to try to work out a lectionary for the Roman Rite that would follow some kind of catechetical scheme and that would cover the major doctrines of the Church in a given period of time. So many of these schemes began with a preconceived theological ordering and picked passages from Scripture that could support the doctrine being treated.

Immediately before the Synod on Catechetics (1977), several Conferences of Bishops tried to deal with the relationship between the cycle of readings and a complete catechetical outline, but all of them seemed to do violence to the scriptural texts. Although one can accept the fact that homilies should also be instructional in nature, one should not say that the whole purpose of a homily is to supply a catechetical need. The role of the homily is indeed more than instructional or didactic.

Nevertheless, given the fact that the homilist must indeed also instruct and would like, too, to cover so many of the doctrines of our faith, it does seem to be advisable to look at the present cycle that is based on the reading of the four Gospels and to see how that structure can lend itself to a study also of the major beliefs of our faith.

Of all of the attempts that I have seen thus far to co-relate the Gospel cycle with a systematic treatment of major doctrinal beliefs, I certainly find the approach of Quentin Quesnell to be the most valid. He has left the cycle in its own integrity and has presented the doctrines of faith in a semisystematic way that does not do violence to either. At times, of course, one can quibble whether or not the exegesis of the biblical passage is total and complete, and at times one can also argue that the major thrust of the passage, taken in itself, may have gone in another direction; nevertheless, the insights that Quesnell offers can be of great help to the homilist who wishes to touch upon most of the doctrinal issues that would be found in any complete catechesis.

It would be my hope that this attempt will inspire other authors to similar projects, that homilists will find therein new insights and fresh approaches to catechesis, and that the relationship between scripture and later dogmatic development will continue to be probed by all of us.

MOST REVEREND REMBERT G. WEAKLAND, O.S.B.
Archbishop of Milwaukee

Chairman of the Bishops' Committee on the
Liturgy (1978–1981)

General Introduction

The Introduction to the *Lectionary for Mass* (Chapter I, Section IX) expresses the wish that, as a result of the new lectionary, "sacred Scripture will become a perpetual source of spiritual life, an important instrument for transmitting Christian teaching and the center of all theological formation." The words are those of Paul VI, and the wish reflects the intentions of the Second Vatican Council. This commentary, in three volumes, is written to help implement that wish.

The commentary tries to show how the lectionary's three-year cycle of Scripture readings can be made the basic instrument for transmitting Christian teaching. It attempts to integrate a complete course of instruction in the basic truths of Catholic faith with the lectionary readings, Sunday by Sunday, through the course of the church year, showing at every point how the truths flow from the Scripture.

To do this, the commentary takes the complete three-year cycle of readings assigned in the lectionary and integrates it with the traditional three-fold division of catechetical instruction: commandments, sacraments, creed. *Commandments* traditionally has covered everything pertaining to morality; *sacraments*, everything about the means of grace: the seven sacraments, other ritual and devotional practices, union with God in prayer; *creed* has been the general heading for the truths of faith: all that Christians believe.

The commentary concentrates on the first of these, morality, during the A Cycle of readings—the readings assigned for 1984, 1987, 1990, and so forth, while are unified around the gospel of Matthew. It concentrates on the second of these,

1

2 : General Introduction

sacraments and prayer, during the B Cycle—the readings assigned for 1985, 1988, 1991, and so forth, centered around the gospel of Mark. It concentrates on the third of these, the Creed, beliefs, during the C Cycle—the readings assigned for 1983, 1986, 1989, and so forth, unified around the gospel of Luke.

The starting point for the reflections of each individual Sunday is always the assigned Scripture reading itself. The commentary is based on an effort to understand the Scripture passage in its full context—historical, critical, and literary, but also ecclesiastical and liturgical. Many questions can be asked about any text of Scripture—more questions than any one book could possibly answer. In this commentary, the questions directed to the text will consistently be, How is this text related to the traditional teachings of the church? During Cycle A (commandments) this means asking, What does this reading tell us about what God wants us to do? During Cycle B (sacraments), what does it tell us about our relationship to God in sacraments, liturgy, sacred places, times, and objects, in ritual and prayer? During Cycle C (Creed), what does it tell us about Christian belief?

Thus the commentary picks out the aspects of each Sunday's reading which shed light upon the over-all theme of the respective year. In the course of the three years, all the traditional basic teachings on morality, sacramentality, and belief (Catholic code, cult, and creed) are exposed in relation to Scripture.

But the book remains a commentary: the order of exposition is scriptural, not dogmatic. There are natural progressions and groupings of material within it, but these flow from the Scriptures themselves and from the choices of Scripture texts offered by the Church. Although the Scripture puts us in touch with all the essentials of Catholic living, and is itself "the soul of all theology" (Vatican II, *Divine Revelation*), still an order of presentation based on Scripture cannot possibly be as systematic as a *Summa Theologiae* or a catechism. A systematic index at the end of each volume will enable users to find what has been treated and where.

General Introduction : 3

Various Uses

Private Reading, Study, and Meditation
This book may be used in many different ways. In itself it is neither a set of ready-made homilies nor conferences, sermons nor instructions. The commentary is intended to be able to be read by any Christian interested in seeing how the Sunday Scripture readings open the biblical heart of Catholic living and teaching.

For the convenience of those who would want to use the book for personal reflection and meditative prayer, the appropriate texts from the lectionary are printed in full before each Sunday's commentary. Those interested in using the book for a fresh approach to the study of theology (perhaps to implement Vatican II, *Priestly Formation*, no. 16) could use it in conjunction with other more systematic expositions of Catholic faith, as described under *Instructions*.

Preaching
At another level, the book could be a source for Sunday homilies. Vatican II (*Liturgy*, no. 52) decreed that "by means of the homily the mysteries of faith and the guiding principles of the Christian life are expounded from the sacred text during the course of the liturgical year." The preacher who has the same audience week by week and would like to follow this directive in preaching to them could consistently use the themes of the expositions in this book, highlight the aspects of each reading featured here and make the basic links with Catholic teaching as they are set forth.

Still, these commentaries are not ready-prepared homilies. They rather furnish the material and suggest the shape and direction of homilies that will be scriptural and doctrinal, yet consistent, coherent, solid, and clear. The preacher must still illustrate the material with appropriate examples, apply it to the special needs of this particular audience, relate it to current questions, contemporary problems, familiar and recent events.

But the link between traditional catechetical teaching and

4 : *General Introduction*

the Sunday Scripture will be provided, so the preacher can give the homily on the day's Scripture and still feel secure that in the course of the year the main tenets of Catholic teaching and practice have been reviewed. Difficulty in combining these two aims of preaching has been reported from many sources in recent years. Some even express a wish for a return to the systematic outlines for diocesan-wide preaching common before Vatican II. But this would violate the instructions of the missal itself that "the homily should develop some point of the readings or of another text from the Ordinary or the Mass of the day."

Instructions

Many pastors report widespread interest in the idea of a course of instructions on the Sunday Scripture readings. Many Catholics would like to give more time to these than the moments at mass. Such a course of instructions could be combined with a general program of instruction to fulfill the demands of the *General Catechetical Directory* for the ongoing formation of adult Catholics. The *Directory* insists on "the need for establishing catechetical cycles which are devoted to a systematic study of the entire Christian message. This organic and well-organized formation is certainly not to be reduced to a simple series of conferences or sermons" (*GCD*, no. 96).

Discussions

The *General Catechetical Directory* recommends, especially with adults, an active method of learning: "Those to be taught, especially if they are adults, can contribute in an active way to the progress of the catechesis. Thus they should be asked how they understand the Christian message and how they can explain it in their own words" (*GCD*, no. 75).

This is particularly useful in a long-term program based on the Sunday Scripture readings. The parishioners could meet to discuss the texts to be read and preached the following Sunday. Various persons could give their understanding of the texts' meanings. But to give a focus to their comments, they might direct them to the questions appropriate to the year of the commentary. In the year of Cycle A, they could ponder the texts, trying to hear what God wants us to do; in year B, asking what the text tells us about the means of grace, prayer, and the sacraments, the possibilities of closer union with God; in the year of Cycle C, they would each try to express what the text reveals to them about what Christians should believe. Then, with the help of the commentary, the further tie-in can be made with "what is taught by the magisterium of the Church" (*GCD*, no. 75).

Building a Unified Parish Life

The fullest possible use of the commentary would be in a parish which had decided to make the Sunday Eucharist, with its Scripture readings and homily, the unifying focus of all parish instruction, activity, and life. The Eucharist is the natural place to look for such a focus. All members of the parish attend Sunday mass. All hear the homilies of the pastor or of the pastoral team. Old and young, liberal and conservative, pious and lukewarm, have this one reality in common. The pastor (or pastoral team) can exploit that fact to build the unity of the parish around the Sunday liturgy.

Here is not the place to discuss the many ways this can be done, including cooperation of many in preparing the liturgy, participation in its music, processions, art work, and the rest; or in linking charitable and social projects of all kinds with the liturgy, so that they lead to it and draw their strength from it, as Vatican II (*Liturgy*, no. 10) postulates. On that, professional liturgists have more to say.

Here the focus must remain on the use of the Scripture lessons from the lectionary. The basic idea would be to have instructions and discussions in the parish, on as many different levels as possible and reaching out to as many members of the parish as possible—in the school, in the individual parish societies, in the parish council, among members of the liturgical committee, the CCD committee, the religious education coordinators and their assistants, the pastors and their ministers, and so forth. All would meet separately some time during the week to preread the three selections assigned for the following Sunday's mass and to reflect on them from the perspective of their own lives, activities, interests, and needs. The discussions and study could be given point and form by being aimed at the general questions proper to each of the three years, as explained above.

Then, some time before the Sunday liturgy, representatives from each of the groups should meet with the pastors and give them some sense of what the week's Scripture has been found to mean for each group. It would then be the task of the pastor to make the Sunday homily a response to all those concerns, insights and misunderstandings, concurring or conflicting needs. The general structures of coordination between Scripture text and traditional teaching, as presented in this commentary, would be most useful in making this attempt.

Method Behind the Commentary

Finally, this commentary gives a concrete example of one valuable way of approaching the Scripture. The details of the comments made are certainly not definitive. There is, for instance, no indispensable connection between the A Cycle and Christian moral teaching. The moral questions can and should some day be put consistently to the B Cycle and the C Cycle as well. Similarly for the sacramental and credal analyses: to write the commentary it was necessary to attach them each to a single year, but there is no reason they could not in future studies be tied to other years. All of Scripture can be queried in various ways and always shows itself "able to instruct you for salvation through faith in Christ Jesus. For all Scripture is inspired by God and is profitable for teaching, for reproof, for correction, and for training in righteousness, that the believer may be complete, equipped for every good work" (2 Timothy 3:15–16).

Introduction to Cycle C

The doctrinal material covered in this commentary on the C Cycle is Catholic dogma as defined in the articles of the Nicene Creed. Fidelity to the content of the Scripture readings Sunday by Sunday has made it impossible to arrange this material in the same order as the articles of the Creed. The complete list of these doctrines as they appear each Sunday is given in the Table of Contents, and a systematic overview of the whole, lined up according to the articles of the Creed, may be found in the Index to the Articles of the Creed.

This commentary is written in particular consciousness of the directives of the *General Catechetical Directory*, in particular of its insistence on the "Christocentrism of Catechesis" (*GCD*, no. 40), the "Trinitarian theocentrism of Catechesis" (*GCD*, no. 41), and the connection of both of these with human existence and ultimate end (*GCD*, no. 42). The commentary observes the "hierarchy of truths to be observed in catechesis":

> The mystery of God the Father, the Son and the Holy Spirit—Creator of all things; the mystery of Christ the Incarnate Word, who was born of the Virgin Mary, and who suffered, died and rose for our salvation; the mystery of the Holy Spirit, who is present in the Church, sanctifying it and guiding it until the glorious coming of Christ, our Savior and Judge; and the mystery of the Church, which is Christ's Mystical Body, in which the Virgin Mary holds the preeminent place." (*GCD*, no. 43)

These are the same truths which the *Directory* then expounds in greater detail in nos. 47 to 54.

8 : Introduction to Cycle C

Those truths are all included in the Creed, and consequently, this commentary, following the example of the *Catechism of the Council of Trent* and of the *Baltimore Catechism,* makes the articles of the Creed its constant dogmatic reference and the focal point of its teaching.

The Creed used here is the one recited by all Catholics at Sunday mass, the Nicene Creed. Because it is heard and spoken so frequently, it has become thoroughly familiar to Catholics today. It includes not only the articles contained in the Apostles' Creed, but also the very important clarifications about the divinity of Christ and the Holy Spirit defined by the church in the fourth-century councils. One article of the Apostles' Creed not explicitly mentioned in the Nicene is "the communion of saints." For completeness that point has been added to the treatment here.

Material on the commandments and virtues, prayer and grace, the sacraments and sacramentals, as explained in the General Introduction, is covered explicitly and in detail in volumes 1 and 2 of this commentary, in connection with Cycle A and Cycle B of the lectionary. Where references to them arise naturally and easily from this year's Scripture readings, they will of course be mentioned here as well. But since the focus of our work this year is not on them, but on the Creed, they will not be listed in the Table of Contents or in the Index to the Articles of the Creed.

The Nicene Creed

We believe in one God,
    the Father, the Almighty,
    maker of heaven and earth,
    of all that is seen and unseen.

We believe in one Lord, Jesus Christ,
    the only Son of God,
    eternally begotten of the Father,
    God from God, Light from Light,
    true God from true God,
    begotten, not made, one in Being with the Father.
    Through him all things were made.
    For us and for our salvation he came down from heaven:
    by the power of the Holy Spirit
        he was born of the Virgin Mary, and became man.
    For our sake he was crucified under Pontius Pilate;
        he suffered, died, and was buried.
        On the third day he rose again
            in fulfillment of the Scriptures;
        he ascended into heaven
            and is seated at the right hand of the Father.
    He will come again in glory to judge the living and the dead,
        and his kingdom will have no end.

We believe in the Holy Spirit, the Lord, the giver of life,
    who proceeds from the Father and the Son.
    With the Father and the Son he is worshiped and glorified.
    He has spoken through the Prophets.
    We believe in one holy catholic and apostolic Church.
    We acknowledge one baptism for the forgiveness of sins.
    We look for the resurrection of the dead,
        and the life of the world to come.

First Sunday of Advent

Reading 1: Jeremiah 33:14–16

Responsorial: Psalm 25:4–5ab, 8–9, 10, 14

Reading 2: I Thessalonians 3:12–4:2

Gospel: Luke 21:25–28, 34–36

He will come . . . to judge the living and the dead

    Today we begin a new liturgical year, a new cycle of Scripture readings, and a new series of reflections. The cycle of readings for this year centers on the gospel according to Saint Luke. That gospel, with the accompanying selections from the Old Testament and the Apostles, sums up the Christian good news of salvation. The same good news has also been summed up by the church in the Creed which we recite at mass each Sunday. As we read the Scriptures this year, we are going to reflect on the relations between the Scripture texts and the articles of the Creed. We will not, however, follow the order of the parts of the Creed but the order of Scripture readings, Sunday by Sunday, and we will always begin from our understanding of the Scriptures. Thus today, following the gospel just read, we consider the phrase in the Creed, "He will come . . . to judge the living and the dead."

    We Christians believe that this life is not for ever. Any sane person must know that. But we believe it. And so we take heed lest our hearts "be weighed down with the cares of this life." We do not want to go blindly into our final day on earth, stumbling into it, like a wild animal into a snare. It is so easy to let ourselves be distracted, dissipated, among the many concerns, interests, distractions, pleasures of our normal lives.

God made this world; he made us and he made our lives. He wants us to live our lives fully, yet to live them in such a way that our end does not come upon us as an unpleasant surprise and a shock. And so we want it to come as something for which we have prepared, in prayer, so that we are ready to stand before the Son of man.

We are aware that when we have put our own last touch to life, have finished our last day, and breathed our last breath, our life comes into judgment. Then and only then can people say for certain what we have made or failed to make of that life of ours.

What will be the final standard of judgment? We know that already. *He* is our standard of judgment. He, Jesus, the Son of man, is the measure against which our lives will be weighed. Does that make us feel guilty already, knowing how far we are from the measure that we should be striving for and growing into? To some extent, yes, of course. But we have no other measure. Christ is the measure. But it takes extraordinary vigilance to keep our life focused on what is truly important and not to allow our hearts to "be weighed down with dissipation and drunkenness and cares of this life." Christ's standard of love, forgiveness, self-sacrifice and service is not an easy one to meet. That is the meaning of "Watch at all times, praying that you may have strength to escape all these things." Jesus is not trying to terrify us. He is trying to make clear how we should live humbly, prayerfully, consciously striving to be "other Christs" in this world.

The thought of death may throw the rest of the world into terror—"distress of nations, men fainting with fear and with foreboding of what is coming." But not us. For judgment on a life like Christ's is vindication. Here is a life worthy of a human being. Here is a life that makes sense. Therefore, "when these things begin to take place," he says, do not be afraid. You "look up and raise your heads, because your redemption is drawing near."

14 : The Season of Advent

The philosopher Socrates had lived a rich and full and beautiful life of service to his fellow citizens. When his death was at hand, he said he felt he had been preparing for this moment all his life. He even felt the approach of death as a redemption. How much more we can feel this, if we have gratefully made use of life as it was given us to be used. At its end, God calls. We answer.

The text speaks of the end of the world. We often feel it would be easy to give our lives to God if we knew for sure that the end of the world was coming soon in this our own lifetime. What we always overlook is that it *is* coming in our own lifetimes.

When our life closes, our world ends. Our individual death is the end of the world for us—forever. That is sufficient reason to prepare, to measure our lives now against Christ's beautiful life, as we profess faith in it in the Creed.

Second Sunday of Advent

Reading 1: Baruch 5:1–9
Responsorial: Psalm 126:1–2ab, 2cd–3, 4–5, 6
Reading 2: Philippians 1:4–6, 8–11
Gospel: Luke 3:1–6

He has spoken through the Prophets.

Today we see John the Baptist begin his preaching. The gospel tells us of John in the wilderness, preaching and exhorting all the people to repentance and baptism for the forgiveness of sins. He does this to prepare them for the coming of the Lord. We read about it now and are reminded of our need for repentance and forgiveness before celebrating the Lord's coming this Christmas.

The gospel reminds us that what we see in John's preaching and what we must experience in our own lives was already described hundreds of years before John in the writings of the great prophet Isaiah. We say in the Creed that we believe in God, the Holy Spirit, "(who) has spoken through the Prophets." This is an example of how the Holy Spirit spoke then through the prophets and of what he said.

> The voice of one crying in the wilderness:
> Prepare the way of the Lord!
> Make his paths straight!

16 : The Season of Advent

That word of the Spirit through the prophet Isaiah is also God's message to us: the Lord is coming, soon, and it is up to us to build for him a royal road to travel on: "Prepare it! Make it straight! Make it level!"

> Every valley shall be filled and every mountain and hill shall be brought low and the crooked shall be made straight and the rough ways shall be made smooth.

In the time that was written, it referred to the salvation of the people in exile. The writer meant that God would come and lead the Hebrews along a smooth road from exile in Babylon to the safe comfort of their own land again. That came true. After they arrived home, they kept the words of the prophecy and made them a part of the holy Scripture. When they read that prophecy in later years, they believed they could hear God telling them that he would come again in just the same way, along just such a broad road, for nothing can ever stand in God's way: "And all flesh shall see the salvation of God."

So when John the Baptist came, preaching the near approach of one who would judge Israel, people began saying, "This too is what God spoke through his prophet Isaiah; he is coming to us now—and all flesh shall see the salvation of God."

The same prophecy is still in our Scriptures. We still read Isaiah in faith, listening for the words of the Spirit spoken to us through him. And so to us today these same words ring: "Prepare the way of the Lord." It is still the voice of one crying in the wilderness. That is, most people pay it no heed. But, to those of us who believe, it is the voice of the Holy Spirit of God we hear through these words, and it is telling us we must prepare.

So with the rest of the Bible. We read it, listening not only for what it said long ago to people in far places, but for what it says to us today. When we do, reading it together, as we do in the church every week, we too begin to feel ourselves touched by God's Holy Spirit, who also speaks and works today through the holy catholic church.

Third Sunday of Advent

Reading 1: Zephaniah 3:14–18a

Responsorial: Isaiah 12:2–3, 4bcde, 5–6

Reading 2: Philippians 4:4–7

Gospel: Luke 3:10–18

one Lord, Jesus Christ, the only Son of God

For us the word "Christ" is not a name; not like Jones or Smith. Christ is a title. Jesus Christ means Jesus the Christ—that is, Jesus the anointed one—or, using an English word that comes from the old Hebrew word for "the anointed one," Jesus the Messiah.

In today's Scripture we see some of what it means to be the Christ: "As the people were in expectation, and all the men questioned in their hearts concerning John, whether perhaps he were the Christ, John answered them all: "I baptize you with water; but he who is mightier than I is coming. . . ."

Why did the people think that perhaps John the Baptist was the Christ? What was the Christ? The Christ was the expected one, anointed by God as had been the kings Saul, David, and Solomon—anointed to save the nation of Israel from its enemies and unite it under a just rule. When the long-expected, long-awaited anointed one, the Messiah, came, God's perfect kingdom would begin, the earth would be at peace, no man, woman, or child would lack for anything. So when John came preaching that all should repent their past selfishness and quarrels, and should right now begin to share all they had with one another, people thought that perhaps he was the Christ. He said, "He who has two coats, let him give one to him who has none"; "He who has two portions of food should give one portion to whoever has none." Could not this be the beginning of the messianic age of justice and peace?

It could be and it was—but John himself was not the Messiah. The real Christ was to come after John: "I am baptizing you with water, but there is one to come who is mightier than I. I am not fit to loosen his sandal strap." But John brought to the people good news: Christ is coming soon.

This Christ was Jesus. Jesus came and fully began God's kingdom on earth—a kingdom of perfect love and sharing. This was his mission, for which he was anointed by God. He called all, as many as wished, to enter his kingdom. But it could not and cannot be entered simply by putting one's name on a list. It has to be entered, we believe, as John preaches—by repentance, by regretting our way of life that has been other than Jesus' way, and by giving up all other ways of life but his.

Moreover, Jesus fulfilled for the world more than the hopes of the coming of the Messiah. He came not only as the Christ, but as "God's only Son, our Lord." The expectations of the prophets, the promises they made, with the Holy Spirit speaking through them, were really expectations of more than just another anointed one like David or Solomon. We read, for instance today in Zephaniah, "Sing aloud, O daughter of Zion, shout, O Israel—for the King of Israel, the Lord, is in your midst": not just another king, but a Messiah who is also the Lord. "Do not fear, O Zion, the Lord your God is in your midst; he will rejoice over you with gladness, he will renew you in his love, he will exult over you with loud singing as on a day of festival." So we believe Jesus is not only our Messiah, our Christ, but is God himself in our midst. He is our Lord, come to us because he loves us and wants to renew us in his love.

We read in the responsorial, "Shout and sing for joy, O inhabitant of Zion, for great in your midst is the holy one of Israel." This is part of the motive of rejoicing which makes this day *Gaudete* Sunday, the Sunday for rejoicing. The Lord is near: Jesus, the Christ, God's only Son, our Lord. He loves us and comes to us to save us. Let us love him in return.

As the second reading says, "Rejoice in the Lord always; again I will say rejoice. The Lord is at hand. And the peace of God, which passes all understanding, will keep your hearts and your minds in Christ Jesus."

Fourth Sunday of Advent

Reading 1: Micah 5:2–5a

Responsorial: Psalm 80:1ac, 2b, 14–15, 17–18

Reading 2: Hebrews 10:5–10

Gospel: Luke 1:39–45

For us and for our salvation
he came down from heaven:
by the power of the Holy Spirit
he was born of the Virgin Mary and became man.

Luke's gospel tells us how Mary received the message from God that she was to be the mother of the Son of God: "The Holy Spirit will come upon you and the power of the most high will overshadow you; therefore the child to be born will be called holy, the Son of God." And Mary said, "Behold I am the handmaid of the Lord; let it be to me according to your word."

Today's selection continues with the story of Mary then going to visit her cousin Elizabeth, the mother of John. Elizabeth recognized Mary as pregnant with a blessed child: "Blessed are you among women, and blessed is the fruit of your womb. And why is this granted me, that the mother of my Lord should come to me?"

So Elizabeth recognizes that the unborn infant whom Mary is carrying is her Lord. So Christ has come, and has begun to make himself known. For he was sent from God to be our

Christ, and to be God in our midst. We believe this. But we also believe that God had a very definite purpose in mind; that Jesus' birth was not in any way an accident, but was God's gift. Thus we read in the letter to the Hebrews, "When Christ came into the world he said: 'Lo, I have come to do thy will, O God'." He came to do his Father's will—and that will was that he should freely give himself for us—"who for us men and for our salvation . . . came down from heaven."

The letter continues: "By that will, we have been sanctified through the offering of the body of Jesus Christ once for all." That is, Christ came into this world in order to do God's will—to give God, in the name of all humankind, an offering such as no one else had ever given or ever could give. Through Christ's self-offering, we can come to the holiness God always intended for us and we can possess the benefits of the kingdom promised by the prophets.

This is the mystery of the redemption. It reaches its high point in the cross and resurrection. But it begins from the very first moment of the incarnation.

Christmas: Mass at Midnight

Reading 1: Isaiah 9:2–4, 6–7

Responsorial: Psalm 96:1–2a, 2b–3, 11–12, 13

Reading 2: Titus 2:11–14

Gospel: Luke 2:1–14

by the power of the Holy Spirit
he was born of the Virgin Mary

The Apostles' Creed says that Jesus was "conceived of the Holy Spirit, born of the Virgin Mary." Christmas is our celebration of that birth.

We say he was born of a *virgin*, to indicate that God is his real Father. Every child is a gift of God, but to say Jesus is born of the *Virgin* Mary is to say that he is purely and completely God's gift to his parents and to all of us. To say "born of the Virgin *Mary*" is to remember that Christ does, however, come from a specific human family. He has ancestors, and through them the history of the human race is his history—just as it is yours and mine. He is human, of flesh, just like us, not a god with ichor in his veins and ambrosia in his mouth, but born a human child, instinctively moving his lips in the sucking motion that reaches out to a mother's milk-filled breasts.

As a real member of the human family, Jesus has a place and a time; he belongs to history and plays his role as one individual in the destiny of peoples. So he is Jewish. Mary was a Jewish girl with the Jewish name of Miriam, the name of the

Christmas Midnight : 23

sister of Moses. She married a tradesman of a small town. She was poor and had to make do with second best—like giving birth to her child in a stable.

Christianity means being somehow enthusiastic about Jesus Christ, but different Christian groups have tried to do that in different ways. Some Christians in the earliest days thought they honored Christ most by stressing that he was human. But that could ignore something else about him that is very important. Against this omission it is useful to remember "born of the *Virgin* Mary"—therefore, truly human, but also truly God's own Son. Others thought they honored Christ most by making him just a god who, like many of the pagan gods, simply put on a human disguise in order to intervene in human affairs. Against this exaggeration, the Creed says, "born of the Virgin *Mary*." He was truly born, and born of a woman, whose name we know, into a family, a place, a nation, which are part of real human history. Like us. Jesus is both man and God; today's Scripture emphasizes that. His parents and he obeyed the regular laws of the civil government. He was born in hard physical circumstances, not wafted down on a soft cloud by smiling angels. But to mark him as God's Son truly—human though he is—angels do sing and proclaim him as Savior. "And Mary remembers all this, and cherishes it in her heart."

Christmas: Mass at Dawn

Reading 1: Isaiah 62:11–12

Responsorial: Psalm 97:1, 6, 11–12

Reading 2: Titus 3:4

Gospel: Luke 2:15–20

*For us and for our salvation
he came down from heaven:
by the power of the Holy Spirit
he was born of the Virgin Mary*

Jesus means Savior. He brings salvation. Today we celebrate the appearance in him of our salvation. The reading from Isaiah says, "Behold your salvation comes." It says that we "shall be called the holy people, the redeemed of the Lord." We shall be called "the ones who are sought out"—sought out by God, who has so loved us that he comes to us to save us.

The message of Christmas is that God loves us and wants our love: "You shall be called a city not forsaken." Look at the refrain from the responsorial psalm: "A light will shine on us; the Lord is born for us." Think of it: the Lord is born for us. *For us*—those are the words of salvation. No matter what problems or evils face us, if the Lord is for us who can be against us? The Lord is for us. He is born for us. He loves us and wants our love. He comes to us in his own Son.

To this the reading from the letter to Titus adds, "When the goodness and loving kindness of God our Savior appeared—

that is, when Christ appeared, for Christ is the goodness of God and the loving kindness of God shown to us, standing before our eyes and ready to offer itself for us—"when the goodness and loving kindness of God our savior appeared, *he saved us.*" And the point is, he saved us by coming to us—not waiting until we came to him. The letter continues: "He saved us, not because of deeds done by us, but in virtue of his mercy."

This is what was made known to the shepherds, when the angels said, "Today is born for you in the city of David a savior who is Christ the Lord." The shepherds believed the message they heard, and they in turn walked to Bethlehem to see "this thing which has happened, which the Lord has made known to us." And they went with haste.

We too believe in order to act on our belief. Our Creed says our Lord "came down from heaven for us and for our salvation, by the power of the Holy Spirit he was born of the Virgin Mary." That is not just something to know like a statement in a history book. That is a message to us: God loves us and he wants our love. Then we too must rise with haste and go to him, that is, respond, give our love in return, and like the shepherds too "make known the saying which has been told us concerning this child." With them we celebrate, "glorifying and praising God for all that we have heard and seen as it had been told us." God is with us. He loves us and he wants our love.

Christmas: Mass During the Day

Reading 1: Isaiah 52:7–10

Responsorial: Psalm 98:1, 2–3ab, 3cd–4, 5–6

Reading 2: Hebrews 1:1–6

Gospel: John 1:1–18

one Lord, Jesus Christ,
the only Son of God,
eternally begotten of the Father,
God from God, Light from Light,
true God from true God, . . .
For us and for our salvation
he came down from heaven:
by the power of the Holy Spirit
he was born of the virgin Mary and became man.

Christmas is the celebration of our Lord's birth. For as the Creed states, he was "eternally begotten of the Father." And he was born of Mary when it became necessary "for us and for our salvation." That is the same thing John's gospel tells us: "In the beginning was the Word and the Word was with God and the Word was God. He was in the beginning with God. . . . And the Word became flesh and dwelt among us . . . and we have beheld his glory, and from his fullness we have all received." He was made known to us, the eternal, invisible God whom "no one has ever seen."

This is indeed a cause for rejoicing. Never think you can understand it, because you cannot. We cannot even see how it would be possible. If anyone had asked us about it before it happened, we would have had to advise against its probability. But it did happen, in God's infinite love and concern for us. He did it. God's own Word, through whom all things were made, now speaks among us, saying, "Love one another as I have loved you." God's own life becomes the light of all people, shines in our darkness and says, "The truth shall make you free."

As the letter to the Hebrews puts it, "In many and various ways God spoke of old to our fathers by the prophets; but in these last days he has spoken to us by his Son, the Son through whom he created the world."

Now of course the whole point of knowing all these things is to make us willing and eager to listen to whatever Jesus says to us. We will do so through the year as we follow the teachings of the Creed, Sunday by Sunday, as they are revealed in the Scripture readings. We listen to him when we read his life in the gospels and ponder again the words written about him by his first followers in the rest of the New Testament. We listen to him when we pray. We listen to him when we go on living in his church with other people who have been struck by this wonderful teaching and decided to try to give their lives to it.

For today we are content just to celebrate the fact that he came, to sing carols, as angels sang in his honor, to give gifts as he has given us so many gifts, to be happy with our family and friends as he has come to be a member of our family and to be our eternal friend.

Holy Family

Reading 1: Sirach 3:2–6, 12–14

Responsorial: Psalm 128:1–2, 3, 4–5

Reading 2: Colossians 3:12–21

Gospel: Luke 2:41–52

and became man

    Today's gospel is a perfect summary of the Christian faith in regard to Jesus. First of all, he is truly a member of the human family, because he has a father and a mother, Joseph and Mary. We usually call Joseph the foster-father of Jesus, because of our Christian belief in Mary's virginal conception and virginal birth. But Mary herself in the gospel does not hesitate to call him Jesus' father: "Your father and I have been looking for you anxiously." The narrator of the gospel calls Joseph and Mary together simply "the parents of Jesus." "The parents of Jesus went up to Jerusalem every year at the feast of Passover. . . . His parents did not know it, but supposed him to be in the company."

    Through Jesus' parents the gospel traces his ancestry back through human history to Adam: "Jesus when he began his ministry was about thirty years of age, being the son (as was supposed) of Joseph, the son of Heli, the son of Matthat . . ." back through David, through Abraham, and all the way to "the son of Enos, the son of Seth, the son of Adam, the son of God."

    Notice that when Luke does this, he begins the line by

saying that Jesus was "as it was supposed" the son of Joseph. So he knows what he is doing when he writes "Jesus' parents" or records Mary's reference to Joseph as "your father." Through Joseph and Mary, Jesus is tied to the whole human race, as each of us is through his or her parents—their parents, eight grandparents, sixteen great-grandparents, and so on, back, back, no one knows how many generations, to the point where all families run together in the common origins of humanity. All human beings are our brothers and sisters—and among these brothers and sisters, bound together in blood, at no matter how great a distance, are Joseph and Mary and Jesus.

But there is another side to Jesus in today's gospel. This same Jesus, at the age of twelve, can say to his father and mother, "How is it you sought me? Did you not know that I must be in my Father's house?" His Father's house is the house of God, the temple, in which they found him. This child of twelve is not merely what he seems. He is able to sit among the teachers of Israel, and able to listen and question as if they were schoolchildren at his feet. When he opens his mouth to speak, those who hear can be amazed "at his understanding and his answers." This is because he is the son of that Father whose house this is. That is because, as the Creed says, he is not only a child of ours, member of our human family: He is also "the only Son of God, eternally begotten of the Father." He is God from God, Light from Light, true God from true God." He is "one in being with the Father."

The two sides of Jesus, the two realities about him, are perfectly portrayed in two lines at the end of the gospel. First, his answer to his mother's rebuke, saying to his earthly parents, "How is it that you sought me? Did you not know that I must be in my Father's house?" Second, the description of what followed: "And he went down with them and came to Nazareth and was obedient to them." He is the Son of the Father who is God of Israel. But he must obey and learn as any other human child.

Moreover, he must grow, just as every human being must: "Jesus increased in wisdom and in stature, in favor with God and man." The eternal Son of God "increased in wisdom"?

How is it possible? It is possible because the eternal Son of God became human. Just as later he will die on a cross, and we will have to say the eternal Son of God died on a cross. Because he became human, everything human is possible: So he could suffer, be afraid, weep, get angry, laugh, have friends whom he loved in the special way of friends; so he could pass from ignorance to knowledge, from the utter inexperience of an infant to the wisdom of a mature, intelligent man. Because he was not only the eternal Son of God, eternally begotten of the Father; he was also human.

He entered a human family, with human parents to place him, date him, train him, teach him the most basic and important things—just as our parents taught us, by word and example. What appeals to us in Jesus as a man was largely the result of what he learned in his own home from the two who gave him those first most powerful lessons in human living. But he remained the Son of the eternal Father, and he came to teach us the way of life.

Solemnity of Mary, Mother of God
(*January 1*)

Reading 1: Numbers 6:22–27

Responsorial: Psalm 67:1–2, 4, 5, 7

Reading 2: Galatians 4:4–7

Gospel: Luke 2:16–21

born of the Virgin Mary

    Mary said in her song of joy, "Behold, from now on all generations will call me blessed." That is what today's feast is about. Mary is the one God has blessed. The heart and soul of that blessing is that he has made her the mother of God. That is why we start with the Old Testament reading about the blessing of Israel.
    The Lord taught the Hebrews how to bless, saying, "The Lord bless you and keep you. . . ." He has indeed blessed Mary and kept her close to him, free from all taint of sin. "The Lord make his face to shine upon you and be gracious to you. . . ." To her he has been gracious above all creatures. She is the one the angel salutes as full of grace—supremely graced by God's graciousness and love. "The Lord lift up his countenance upon you and give you peace." "The spirit of the Lord came upon her and the power of the most high overshadowed her." He gave her peace—the one born of her is the

prince of peace. The Lord promises, "So shall they put my name upon the people of Israel and I will bless them." Mary confesses, "Behold from henceforth all generations shall call me blessed."

So we pray in the psalm, "May God bless us in his mercy." How he blessed us is shown in the second reading: "When the time had fully come, God sent forth his Son, born of a woman, born under the law, to redeem those who were under the law. . . ." Our blessing is the gift she received for us, with which she was graced: Jesus, God, the prince of peace, who comes to us "born of a woman."

We have been meditating these last several Sundays on the mystery of Christ himself, who in showing us the perfection of our humanity, shows us what we might have hope of becoming; but who is also true God as he is true man. We have marveled at the profundity and simplicity of this mystery. It means that God loves us and comes to us. It means that God is one of us, and we are brothers and sisters of God. It means that a perfect man has once existed: but that man was perfect because he was more than a man—he was God's eternal son.

We have seen how various groups of Christians in their enthusiasm for one side or the other of Christ's rich and powerful personality have overemphasized one feature to the denial of others, and in so doing have put the true Christian tradition into jeopardy. Jesus is not our Savior if he is not truly God, of one nature with the Father. But it is hard to take the whole picture of Jesus Christ together, keeping our eye directly on the mystery. There is a constant temptation to pick and choose among the many aspects of the riches of Christ. That is why the church from as early as the fifth century found for itself a simpler way. Instead of remembering formulas and definitions, one can preserve a true and faithful picture of what the Creed teaches about Jesus if one holds to the title that is honored in today's liturgy—if one remembers that Mary is the mother of God.

Why does this tie everything correctly together? Because if God had a mother, then God must have been truly human. God—just God in himself—has no mother, could not possibly have one. But God become man must have a mother or he would not truly be human. And that is the other side of the story. That is, if Jesus was just God appearing in a human disguise, he would have no mother. He would have made for himself a fictitious body, or cast a spell over the eyes of people who met him so they would see a body where none existed.

But if God wanted to be a human like ourselves, then God needed a body formed in the womb of a woman; made not of the fifth essence, as some philosophers would have it, but made of the flesh and blood of another human person. You can build a doll or a robot and it might look like a human being, but to be the genuine article, it must be born.

And so the test of your faith in Jesus' humannness is whether or not you believe he was really born of a woman, whether he really had a mother. There were some who thought that it would dishonor God to have lived inside a woman's body and to have been introduced into human society by the humble process of normal human birth. But that is what is involved in becoming human . . . and God did it.

The other test of what you believe about Jesus is whether you do or do not accept him as truly God's eternal Son. If you do, you must say of that mother—of Mary—that she is the mother of God. This then is why the church finally saw and decided in the fifth century that the safeguard against all the Christ-heresies would be to remember that Mary was the mother of God, and to honor her regularly under that title. And that is what we are doing today.

Second Sunday after Christmas

Reading 1: Sirach 24:1–2, 8–12

Responsorial: Psalm 147:12–13, 14–15, 19–20

Reading 2: Ephesians 1:3–6, 15–18

Gospel: John 1:1–18

God from God, Light from Light,
true God from true God,
begotten, not made, one in Being with the Father

The three readings today again concentrate on the message of the incarnation: God himself became one of us. The gospel is the most direct: "The Word became flesh and dwelt among us." What word is that? "In the beginning was the Word, and the Word was with God, and the Word was God." The one who became flesh and dwelt among us, Jesus Christ: he was the word who was in the beginning, was with God, and was God. "All things were made through him. In him was life, and the life was the light of men. The light shines in the darkness, and the darkness has not overcome it."

This is the basis of the expressions we use in the Creed: that our Lord, Jesus Christ, is "God from God, Light from Light, true God from true God; begotten not made, one in being with the Father." For "in the beginning was the Word, and the Word was with God, and the Word was God. . . . [He was] the true light that enlightens every man . . .; the only Son, who is in the bosom of the Father."

Second Sunday after Christmas : 35

The reading from the letter to the Ephesians says that God the Father chose us in Christ before the foundation of the world. That means that Christ was with God the Father before the foundation of the world: "God from God, Light from Light, true God from true God." Moreover, because he is light from light, and enlightens every person, and his life is the light of all, Paul can pray to "the Father of glory, the God and Father of our Lord Jesus Christ, that he give a spirit of wisdom and of revelation in the knowledge of Christ, that we may have the eyes of our hearts enlightened by him and know the great things to which he has called us."

Christ the eternal word, Christ the light of our lives, goes by still another name: he is called wisdom, the eternal wisdom of God. Here the text is from the Old Testament book of Sirach, and strictly speaking it is about created wisdom, not about the uncreated word and wisdom of God. Still, the created wisdom points to Christ the uncreated, and so we think of him as we read that wisdom was created "from eternity, in the beginning . . . for eternity I shall not cease to exist." We read that wisdom, like Christ, was told to "make your dwelling in Jacob, in Israel receive your inheritance." One can say that Christ as truly as wisdom, "ministered in the holy tabernacle . . . was established in Zion . . . rested finally in Jerusalem."

This created wisdom is of course the law which God gave to Israel. As the psalm says, "He declares his word to Jacob; his statutes and ordinances to Israel." Israel was proud and happy with reason; God had favored them with his law: "He has not dealt thus with any other nation; they do not know his ordinances." It is indeed wonderful. And yet, how much more does John's gospel say of Christ: "The law was given through Moses; grace and truth came through Jesus Christ."

Finally, as the perfect incarnation of the word of God, Jesus is the one perfect revelation on this earth of what God is really like. He is "God from God, Light from Light, true God from true God." Yet we can see him, listen to him, study him, touch him—as we can crucify him: "And the Word became flesh and dwelt among us, full of grace and truth; we have beheld his glory, glory as of the only Son from the Father." As John wrote in his first epistle,

That which was from the beginning, which we have heard, which we have seen with our eyes, which we have looked upon and touched with our hands, concerning the word of life—the life was made manifest, and we saw it, and testify to it, and proclaim to you the eternal life which was with the Father and was made manifest to us—that which we have seen and heard we proclaim also to you, so that you may have fellowship with us; and our fellowship is with the Father and with his Son Jesus Christ.

Epiphany

Reading 1: Isaiah 60:1–6

Responsorial: Psalm 72:1–2, 7–8, 10–11, 12–13

Reading 2: Ephesians 3:2–3a, 5–6

Gospel: Matthew 2:1–12

one holy catholic and apostolic Church

The title "Christ," we have seen, means "anointed one," and is taken from an Old Testament title for the kings of Israel. We believe that Jesus was indeed anointed to be king of Israel, king of the Jews. That is the title that was written over his head on the cross. That is the promise the angel Gabriel spoke to Mary before his birth: "The Lord God will give him the throne of his father David, and he will rule in the house of Jacob forever." That is the title by which the wise men from the East ask for him in today's gospel: "Where is he who has been born king of the Jews?"

Nevertheless, today's celebration takes that fact about Jesus only as a beginning. "Epiphany" means that Jesus is not only king of Israel, but king, Messiah, Christ, and Savior to every land, people, and nation throughout the world. Jesus was a Jew. But he is Savior of the world. That is why the wise men come looking for him: "We have seen his star in the East and have come to worship him." The gospel does not even tell us what country or countries the Magi were from—just from somewhere "in the East." But the gospel tells of their coming as a representative sample of all the nations of the world. So the psalm says, "May the kings of Tarshish and of the isles render him tribute, may the kings of Sheba and Seba bring gifts. May all kings fall down before him, all nations serve him." The reading from the letter of Paul to the Ephesians declares that "the Gentiles are fellow heirs"; that is, all the non-Jewish peoples of the world shall join with God's chosen people, the Jews, and shall be along with them heirs of the great fathers, Abraham, Isaac, and Jacob. Gentiles shall be "members of the same body" with them, "partakers of the promise in Christ Jesus through the gospel." Paul says this is a mystery now revealed—for anyone reading the Old Testament before this revelation would almost certainly have had the impression that the promises were only for the Jews.

Still, many Old Testament texts, like the one in the first reading from Isaiah, suggest that the full story is that God comes first to Israel, then to the other nations of the world as well: "The Lord will arise upon you, and his glory will be seen upon you," that is, upon Israel. And then,

> And nations shall come to your light, and kings to the brightness of your rising . . . the wealth of the nations shall come to you; a multitude of camels shall cover you; the young camels of Median and Ephah, all those from Sheba shall come. They shall bring gold and frankincense, and shall proclaim the praise of the Lord

That is what today's feast celebrates. We are the gentiles, the nations of the world. Because God came in flesh within the nation of Israel, we turn to him there. Because Jesus died in Jerusalem, we turn our thoughts and hearts to him there. Centering on what happened once in that nation and in that holy city, we form one church around the world.

The Creed says Christ came to be Christ, king, Savior, not for one nation alone but for all the world: "who for us and for our salvation came. . . ." And so the one body of Christ, of which Paul writes, is formed of all nations together and makes one church around the world. As the Creed says, "We believe in one holy *catholic*"—that is, universal, around the world, for all nations, lands, and peoples, for every social class, for every individual human person—"and apostolic church" centered on one Savior, Lord, and Christ.

Baptism of the Lord

Reading 1: Isaiah 42:1–4, 6–7
Responsorial: Psalm 29:1–2, 3ac–4, 3b, 9b–10
Reading 2: Acts 10:34–38
Gospel: Luke 3:15–16, 21–22

the Holy Spirit, the Lord, the giver of life
one baptism for the forgiveness of sins

    Today's gospel is a manifestation of the blessed trinity; three divine persons, each of whom is God. The Father reveals himself in a voice from heaven; the Holy Spirit shows himself in bodily form as a dove, coming upon Jesus; and it is Jesus to whom the voice from heaven is directed: "Thou art my beloved Son; with thee I am well pleased." The occasion of this special manifestation of God in all three divine Persons is clearly a very important moment in the life of Jesus. It is the scene of his baptism; the event to which today's liturgical celebration is devoted.
    Jesus was baptized by John the Baptist in what John called his baptism of repentance. People were coming to John, making a confession of sin, and entering the Jordan river to be washed as a sign of putting off the old life with its sinfulness. John said that the Christ who was coming after him would baptize people with the Holy Spirit and with fire. But when

Jesus first came he did no baptizing. He came in the long line of repentant sinners who approached John, even though he himself had no sin to confess. When Jesus was baptized by John, the manifestation occurred: the heavens opened and the Holy Spirit descended upon him in bodily form, and a voice came from heaven: "Thou art my Beloved Son."

This manifestation of the Trinity underlined the decisive importance of the moment of baptism, and marked the beginning of the baptism with the Spirit which was to begin with Jesus. This is the baptism which has come to us: the baptism Christ founded, which is given in the name of the three Persons of God: "I baptize you in the name of the Father and of the Son and of the Holy Spirit," we say. It is the baptism which not only symbolizes our repentance, our desire to wash away the past. It also symbolizes God's actual forgiveness of all our sins. And as a result of it we actually receive what is symbolized. We do receive forgiveness of sins in baptism, and that perfect forgiveness remains accessible to us all our lives because we also receive the Holy Spirit at baptism. God's grace and love are poured forth in our hearts by the Holy Spirit which is given to us.

And so we pray in the main prayer of this mass that we, as God's children, born to him of water and the Spirit, may remain faithful to our great calling which we received in baptism. We ask that we who share Christ's humanity may also come to share in his divinity. We pray that we who share in the sonship of Christ—so that God's voice could now say of us, "These are my beloved sons and daughters"—may "follow in Christ's path of service to man, and reflect the glory of his kingdom even to the ends of the earth."

The connection is given in the first reading from Isaiah: God said to Jesus, "Thou art my beloved son, with thee I am well pleased." Isaiah presents God as speaking and saying, "Behold my servant, my chosen, in whom my soul delights"; "I have put my spirit upon him," and the Spirit does come upon Jesus in the gospel's baptism scene. And the reason for this gift of the Spirit is, according to Isaiah, to enable him to do great works of love:

> He will bring forth justice to the nations. A bruised reed he will not break, and a dimly burning wick he will not quench; he will faithfully bring forth justice. He will not fail or be discouraged till he has established justice on earth. . . . I have called you in righteousness, I have taken you by the hand and kept you. I have given you as a covenant to the people, a light to the nations, to open the eyes that are blind, to bring out the prisoners from the dungeon, from the prison those who sit in darkness. . . .

It is this life in the Spirit which we pray to share as the natural, expected fulfillment of our life after baptism. This is the full meaning of "we acknowledge one baptism for the forgiveness of sins." It is not just for forgiveness of all our past sins. It is also for a new life which is the opposite of a life of sin, and which tends to undo all the evil effects of sin in the world. It is for a life of love and service like Christ's. This life we achieve in the Holy Spirit who is given to us in baptism. As we say in the creed, "We believe in the Holy Spirit, the Lord, the giver of life. . . ." This is the true life which he gives: the life which Christ led.

The reading from Acts says that this life began—began at least in a fashion which all the world could see—"after the baptism which John preached: how God anointed Jesus of Nazareth with the Holy Spirit and with power; and he went about doing good and healing all that were oppressed by the devil, for God was with him." This is the life to which we have been called, that has been opened to us in our baptism, which forgave us our sins, lifted us from the world of sinfulness, and blessed us with the power and the life of the Holy Spirit, the Lord, the giver of life.

Second Sunday of the Year

Reading 1: Isaiah 62:1–5

Responsorial: Psalm 96:1–2a, 2b–3, 7–8a, 9–10ac

Reading 2: 1 Corinthians 12:4–11

Gospel: John 2:1–12

the Holy Spirit, the Lord, the giver of life

In the readings for Epiphany and, last Sunday, for the baptism of the Lord, we have been considering Scripture texts that speak of how Christ first began to be known to all the world: being honored by the wise men from the East, being proclaimed God's Son by the dove and the voice from heaven. At the same time we have been considering the role of the Holy Spirit in the Christian life, which is the fulfillment of baptism. Both these themes continue in this Sunday's liturgy, which is still part of the long introduction to the church's year.

Today's gospel therefore tells us of the first of Jesus' signs, which he "did at Cana in Galilee and manifested his glory; and his disciples believed in him." This miracle, producing wine for a wedding celebration, is a good illustration of our faith that the things of this world are created by God. One of the most persistent errors in the first centuries of Christianity was the teaching that this world was not created by the true God, the Father of our Lord Jesus Christ, but by some lesser spirit or demon. This idea was central for the Marcionites, for various Gnostic groups, and, in a further advanced form, for the Manicheans. The adherents of these sects, from the second through the fifth centuries, had severe problems accepting the goodness of this material universe. What pertained to the flesh, and in particular normal human love and marriage, was to them an abomination.

But the orthodox Christian faith was and is that God made the world, that God loves the world he made, and that, as Father, he gives us the good things of creation for our comfort and joy. He wants us to be happy.

In the gospel, six jars of water, each holding twenty or thirty gallons, are found filled with wine. That amount of wine would fill six hundred to nine hundred standard-size modern wine-bottles. This is what Jesus provided for the guests after they had finished the wine that was given them originally! Clearly Jesus is no Puritan, no Manichean! His Father, the one true God, is the same God who made "heaven and earth (and) all that is seen and unseen." He himself is the Son, "through whom all things were made."

Joy in the good things God has made for us is typical of true Christianity. Jesus attends a wedding feast and blesses all marriage by his presence. Jesus' mother shows a kind solicitude that the wedding should be a happy celebration. Mary notices and quickly turns to her son for help when "there is no more wine."

The same spirit appears in the selection from Isaiah, where the great delight of God in a faithful people is said to be like the delight a bridegroom has in his bride: "For the Lord delights in you, and your land shall be married. For as a young man marries a virgin, so shall your Builder marry you; and as the bridegroom rejoices over the bride, so shall your God rejoice over you."

Our life in this world is, after baptism, life in the Spirit. The reading from 1 Corinthians stresses the fact that all forms of life and of service are gifts of the Spirit, the Lord and giver of life:

> There are varieties of gifts, but the same Spirit. . . . To each is given the manifestation of the Spirit for the common good. To one is given through the Spirit the utter-

ance of wisdom, to another knowledge according to the same Spirit, to another faith by the same Spirit, to another gifts of healing by the one Spirit,

and so the working of miracles, prophecy, and discernment of spirits, various kinds of tongues, interpretations of tongues. Paul lists the various ministries which were performed in the church of his day and says, "All these are inspired by one and the same Spirit, who apportions to each one individually as he wills."

And so we see more of what is meant by "the Holy Spirit, the Lord, the giver of life." He gives our life to us, especially our Christian life. Our works for one another in community are manifestations of the Spirit; ways in which he shows himself as Lord and giver of life.

We say we have seen Christ—whereas of course we have never seen him physically. The first generation of Christians saw him with their own eyes. Moreover, as John's gospel tells us, "no one had ever seen God the Father." But the Spirit, whom we think of as eminently invisible, is, as a matter of fact, the divine Person of whom we have the most direct experience; for he manifests himself continually in all the works that go to the building up of our Christian community. That is why in the Creed, what we say about life, church, baptism, forgiveness, hope of resurrection, all stand under the name of the Spirit in the third part of the Creed, just as creation stands in the first part of the Creed under the name of the Father and Christ's life for our redemption stands in the second part under the name of the Son.

Third Sunday of the Year

Reading 1: Nehemiah 8:1–4a, 5–6, 8–10

Responsorial: Psalm 19:7, 8, 9, 14

Reading 2: 1 Corinthians 12:12–30

Gospel: Luke 1:1–4, 4:14–21

He has spoken through the Prophets

one . . . Church

by the power of the Holy Spirit . . . born of the Virgin Mary

   We continue our consideration of the being and works of the Holy Spirit. The Holy Spirit is truly God, just as the Father is God and the Son is God. The special manifestation of the Spirit among us, we have seen, is in the works of the Christian community. The Spirit is given in baptism; the Spirit prompts the love of Christ in our hearts; the Spirit makes us members of the one body of Christ in the world, helping us, through his gifts, to do our special tasks in the body; and it is the Spirit who gives the gifts which we give to one another.

   The Creed also says of the Spirit, "He has spoken through the prophets." This refers to the great work of the Spirit which is the inspiration of Scripture. We say that the Bible is inspired by God. That means it comes from God's Spirit, is full of God's Spirit, and breathes that very Spirit into us when we read it. So in the first reading today, we see how the books of the law of Moses—the first five books of the Bible—are rediscovered by the people of Israel when they return to their land after the exile. They find these books and Ezra the scribe reads them in the sight of all the people: "And when he opened the book, all the people stood. And Ezra blessed the Lord, and all the people answered, 'Amen, Amen,' bowing their heads and worshiping the Lord." Ezra read from the book and explained it and all the people mourned that they had not observed God's laws. But Ezra told them to rejoice, because now they had found God's word and this day of their finding was a day holy to the Lord.

In this spirit the psalm sings, "Your words, Lord, are spirit and life . . ." and praises the law of the Lord as perfect, the precepts of the Lord as right, the ordinances of the Lord as true— all different expressions for the sacred Scriptures of Moses, the law of the Lord. The Scripture is the work of the Spirit—"(who) has spoken through the prophets," whose words and writings the Scriptures contain.

How the writing of the Scriptures actually took place we see from today's gospel selection, which opens with the short preface to the gospel of Luke. Luke wrote his gospel, we believe, under the inspiration of the Spirit. But inspiration is not something magic that comes to the writer of a book of the Bible like a voice from the clouds. The writer of what will become part of the Bible puts down, like any other writer, what he or she knows or has experienced or learned or heard or imagined.

Luke begins, "Inasmuch as many have undertaken to compile a narrative of the things which have been accomplished among us . . . it seemed good to me also, having followed all things closely for some time past, to write an orderly account." So Luke knows of others who have written just as he is about to write. And he says he has studied up on these matters— "having followed all things closely." He does not mean that he was present as an eyewitness when these things happened, because he was not. Luke was not one of the original disciples. In fact, he clearly says the things he is going to write "have been delivered to us by those who from the beginning were eyewitnesses and ministers of the word. . . ."

Before Luke were the original eyewitnesses and then there

were the preachers, the ministers of the word, those who recounted in story-form what the eyewitnesses had seen. Many conclude that Luke must have belonged to at least the second and probably even the third generation of Christians. He had heard the preaching of the life and teaching of Christ, preaching based on eyewitness accounts of a preceding generation, and he had read accounts of the gospel by others—even by many. Now he was going to write an orderly account of his own. This work of his was, we believe, a work of the Spirit, especially inspired so that Luke's gospel can be read by us as the word of God.

Then in the gospel passage about the first preaching of Jesus we see again the reverence for the written word of God. Jesus himself stands in the synagogue and reads from the prophet Isaiah. What he reads are Isaiah's words of how the Spirit of God has come upon him, anointing him "to preach good news to the poor, to proclaim release to the captives and recovery of sight to the blind, to set at liberty those who are oppressed, to proclaim the acceptable year of the Lord." These too then are works of the Spirit, who anoints God's chosen one to do these good things. Jesus declares that the Spirit has anointed him in that way. He says, "This scripture has been fulfilled in your hearing."

Finally, the whole of the passage from Paul's letter to the Corinthians is a picture of the work of the Spirit: "By one Spirit we were all baptized into one body— Jews or Greeks, slaves or free—and all were made to drink of one Spirit." This Spirit, Paul explains, gives different tasks to each of us, as each part of one body has a different function, yet all work together for the good of the whole. So "God has appointed in the church apostles, prophets, teachers, workers of miracles, healers, helpers, administrators, speakers in various kinds of tongues. . . ." And all are united in one body and work together and help one another as a result of the one Spirit whom all received in baptism. Therefore, "we believe in the Holy Spirit, the Lord, the giver of life . . . he has spoken through the Prophets. We believe in one holy catholic and apostolic Church. We acknowledge one baptism for the forgiveness of sins."

The Spirit's action on us reflects the Spirit's action on Jesus himself, for we also say in the same creed, "By the power of the Holy Spirit, he was born of the Virgin Mary and became man . . . was crucified . . . suffered, died and was buried . . . rose again in fulfillment of the Scriptures; he ascended into heaven and is seated at the right hand of the Father." Of his whole life it was true that "the Spirit of the Lord is upon me; therefore he has anointed me, sent me. . . ."

Fourth Sunday of the Year

Reading 1: Jeremiah 1:4–5, 17–19

Responsorial: Psalm 71: 1–2, 3–4a, 5–6ab, 15ab, 17

Reading 2: 1 Corinthians 12:31–13:13

Gospel: Luke 4:21–30

who proceeds from the Father and the Son

We continue to reflect on the works of the Holy Spirit. The reading from Jeremiah illustrates again how the Spirit "has spoken through the prophets." It portrays the call of Jeremiah to be a prophet. God says he chose him before he was born: "Before I formed you in the womb I knew you and before you were born I consecrated you, and appointed you a prophet to the nations." Jeremiah is told that in the power of the Spirit, he will be able to resist the most powerful enemies: "They will fight against you, but they shall not prevail against you, for I am with you, says the Lord, to deliver you." Now God says this to us as well through his Holy Spirit abiding in us. God makes this come true. We have the strength to fulfill the callings he has given us, to live up to the ideals he proposes to each of us.

The greatest ideal is described in today's selection from 1 Corinthians. That ideal is the heart of the Christian life, and is the most special work of the Holy Spirit. In 1 Corinthians 12, Paul writes about the greatest of the gifts of the Spirit; greater even than the theological virtues of faith and hope. The greatest of all gifts is love. He tells us it is more than being a prophet, more than having all gifts of knowledge.

For love, Paul says, never ends. It is the essence of our Christian life in heaven forever. Other spiritual gifts are for a time and for a particular place, to make up a certain deficiency, a passing need. Even faith and hope, wonderful as they are, are like that: we need them only because we do not actually as yet see the great spiritual realities in which we believe and for which we hope. But love does not exist to make up a deficiency. Love is what it is all about. God is love. And the chief work of the Spirit, the Lord and giver of life, is to dwell in our hearts as the Spirit of love, giving us a share in the perfect love which is God himself.

By giving us a share in that love, the Spirit creates the church, the community of love. By that love in particular the Spirit makes that church a holy church, for this is the essence of holiness: to live in love. If "we believe in one holy catholic . . . Church," it is because we believe that love should unite all human beings around the world, and because we accept the fact that love is actually something more than human; it is a gift of God, given through his Spirit.

The Spirit is the spirit of love because he "proceeds from the Father and the Son." The Son is the eternal image of the Father, the perfect reflection of the Father. From these two together, perfect Father, perfect Son, each perfect with the infinite beauty of God, there proceeds a perfect love. This perfect love is the complete and perfect self-expression of them both, and of them both mutually. That is the love given to us, in which we share in God's own life.

Notice how the prayer of today's mass is a special prayer for a greater share of that perfect love: "Help us to love you with all our hearts and to love all men as you love them. . . . You have formed us a people in the image of your Son . . . may we show love for one another even as you have loved us."

Fifth Sunday of the Year

Reading 1: Isaiah 6:1–2a, 3–8

Responsorial: Psalm 138:1–2a, 2bcd–3, 4–5, 7d–8

Reading 2: 1 Corinthians 15:1–11

Gospel: Luke 5:1–11

born . . . suffered, died . . . buried . . . rose

The call of the prophet Isaiah is portrayed in the first reading. First the prophet is burned pure of his sins: "Behold this has touched your lips; your guilt is taken away and your sins forgiven." Then he is given a mission: " 'Whom shall I send?' 'Send me!' "

The mission of the Old Testament prophet was to speak God's word in the power of the Spirit. In the New Testament we hear of the special missions received by the apostles to preach the gospel of Jesus Christ. Today's reading from Paul's letter to the Corinthians tells what that mission meant to Paul and reminds us of the heart of the gospel which we have received through this preaching. Paul says he delivered to his hearers as of first importance that which he himself had once received: that Christ died for our sins in accordance with the Scriptures, that he was buried, that he was raised on the third day according to the Scriptures, and that he appeared to those who had known him in life, and to some others. This is what he preached in the power and grace of the Spirit. This is the Christian gospel. Christ suffered, died, rose from the dead, has shown himself to many witnesses, and in all this those Scriptures are fulfilled which promised our salvation.

But this list of events is the very structure of the second part of our Creed. In the Creed we do not recite all the things that happened to Jesus through his whole lifetime, nor go through all the wonderful things he taught. We simply remind ourselves of the most important facts we believe. First we recall who he was: the Son of God who "was born of the Virgin Mary and became man." Then we recall what he did: "for our sake he was crucified under Pontius Pilate, suffered, died and was buried. On the third day he rose again in fulfillment of the Scriptures; he ascended into heaven and is seated at the right hand of the Father." This is the message about Christ, just as we learned it when we were children. And in this letter of Paul, written before the year 60, this is exactly what he says he has been preaching and teaching, because this is also exactly what he himself had received. This is, he writes to those early Christians and to us, "The gospel which you received, in which you stand, by which you are saved if you hold it fast."

Moreover, this little story of who Jesus is and of what happened to him is the outline of the church's year of worship. Every year we remember Jesus' coming and birth through Advent, Christmas, and Epiphany seasons; Jesus' resurrection and glorification through Easter and Pentecost. In fact, every mass, of every Sunday and every day, is a memorial of Jesus' suffering and death, an act of faith in his resurrection, a looking forward to his coming again, and so another reminder of the gospel "by which you are saved if you hold it fast."

These are the great salvation events. They really happened in one person, Jesus. And they are the pattern of what is happening and what is going to happen to each of us.

In 1986 and 1989, this is the last Sunday before Lent. For the readings of the next and following Sundays in those years, turn to the Lenten series.

Sixth Sunday of the Year

Reading 1: Jeremiah 17:5–8

Responsorial: Psalm 1:1–2, 3, 4, 6

Reading 2: 1 Corinthians 15:12, 16–20

Gospel: Luke 6:17, 20–26

*We look for the resurrection of the dead,
and the life of the world to come.*

Last week we looked particularly closely at the passage of 1 Corinthians, in which Paul tells of the essential gospel message which he preached: that Christ suffered, died, rose from the dead, and that this is the fulfillment of all the Old Testament promises for our salvation. In the second reading for today's liturgy, we continue with that passage from Paul's letter.

Paul begins to clarify what it means to say we find salvation in what happened in Christ. Because Christ rose, we too shall rise. Those who have fallen asleep—that is, who have died—in Christ, have not perished. They will rise again. Because we know Christ has been raised, we are no longer trapped in our sins, helplessly caught in the hopeless, ever-recurring pattern of sin, decay, and death. In Christ we can and do find the way to a life that escapes the bounds of self in perfect love, and this is the way to eternal life.

We look forward to this as the greatest work of God in his world, the final fulfillment of all the scriptural promises. "We look for the resurrection of the dead and the life of the world to come." We shall live again. Christ returned from the dead as "the first fruits of those who have fallen asleep"; that is, he will be the first among many. We are among those many.

What a different picture of the world results from a sincere faith in these promises. The selection from the prophet Jeremiah confirms this when it tells us where those who are wise will put their trust: "Blessed is the man who trusts in the Lord. He is like a tree planted by the water that sends out its roots in the stream, that does not fear when drought and heat come, that remains ever green, bringing forth fruit." This trust without fear is the lot of those who know that our future depends on God alone, and that God has shown us in Christ the future he has in mind for us.

On the other hand, in the light of this future, how foolish and sad, even—as the Scripture says—how "cursed is the man who trusts in man, who makes flesh his arm, whose heart turns away from the Lord. He is like a shrub in the desert. He shall dwell in the parched places of the wilderness, in an uninhabited salt land." For everything short of God on which we may think we can depend will fade and fall away. It contains no water of eternal life welling up within it. But God does. He alone endures—and he invites us to choose life and so to be with him forever.

It is with this "life of the world to come" in mind, this need of putting our trust, hope, values, in the right place, that Jesus speaks the words in today's gospel. They are the introduction to the Great Sermon, the one we know from Matthew's gospel as the Sermon on the Mount. In Luke the contrast between Christ's values and the world's values is even more strongly emphasized for us: "Blessed are you poor . . . you that hunger now . . . you that weep now; blessed are you when men hate you . . . exclude you . . . revile you . . . cast out your name as evil." That's when you're lucky, happy, well-off. Why? Because this life is not the definitive life. We look for "the resurrection of the dead and the life of the world to come." In that life, you poor shall possess "the kingdom of God . . . you that hunger now . . . shall be satisfied . . . you that weep now . . . shall laugh." And you whom all hate, exclude, revile, cast out on account of the Son of man, you will have a great reward in heaven . . . for this is the way it always is with the true prophets. The world will sense your commitment to Christ's cause and will make you pay for it.

On the other hand, if you make peace with this world, settling into a comfortable situation, making your long-term plans for a secure future which the world can appreciate and admire, then, "Woe to you that are rich, for you have received your consolation. Woe to you that are full now, for you shall hunger. Woe to you that laugh now, for you shall mourn and weep." The life of the world to come is a life according to God's standards and norms. These are often the direct reverse of the values of this world.

Is everyone satisfied with your view of religion? Then you may be overlooking some important part of the message. For "woe to you when all men speak well of you, for so their fathers did to the false prophets." A picture of Christianity that is fairly generally acceptable, that does not much disturb the world as it is, may not quite be the kind of Christianity Jesus had in mind.

In 1983, this is the last Sunday before Lent. For the readings of the next and following Sunday, turn to the Lenten series.

Seventh Sunday of the Year

Reading 1: 1 Samuel 26:2, 7–9, 12–13, 22–23

Responsorial: Psalm 103:1–2, 3–4, 8, 10, 12–13

Reading 2: 1 Corinthians 15:45–49

Gospel: Luke 6:27–38

For us and for our salvation . . . crucified

This Sunday continues the study of the Great Sermon, which sums up the heart of Jesus' preaching in the gospel of Luke. It contains sayings which from the earliest days were considered among the most striking, the best remembered, the most characteristic ideas people had from Jesus. We have heard them often, but they strike us again every time we listen to them. Not that we live by them. But at least, we do know in our hearts we cannot ignore them. They challenge us, for one thing, because they are so unfortunately clear. There is no mystery about these lines; the ideas are not hidden under any figure. A child can make them out, and can see how beautiful is the life they sketch. But few and far are the souls who really resolve in their hearts to try to do just what they say.

Yet the very existence of these words in the gospel makes a difference in our lives, even if it does not determine in detail the course of our living. At least we are aware at some level that as Christians our standards, norms, measures cannot be the same as those of the rest of the world. We know we are called to something much more serious, much greater.

With such thoughts in mind, we listen again to the gospel words: "Love your enemies; do good to those who hate you; bless those who curse you; pray for those who abuse you." To love and do good to those who hate you, those who are your enemies. Is civilized life conceivable in these terms? No self-defense? No wars? No lawsuits? Just love and do good to those who run into your car? rob your house? murder your child?

Jesus answers, "To him who strikes you on the cheek, offer the other also. From him who takes away your cloak, do not withhold your coat as well." Can he be serious? Well, the Great Sermon is very solemnly introduced, is placed in a very central, prominent place in the gospel, seems to have been put together as a summary presentation of what Christianity is all about; and is among the parts of Jesus' teaching most remembered and quoted in the earliest Christian writings.

"Give to everyone who begs of you. . . . If you lend to those from whom you hope to receive, what credit is that to you? Even sinners lend to sinners to receive as much again." What is the basis of these norms? Are they more than just a pious exhortation? Have they anything to do with our essential belief as expressed in the Creed? They have everything to do with the Creed. The norm of action here proposed is precisely the action we believe God has exercised toward us. Jesus, "for us and for our salvation," when we were yet sinners, "for our sake," became man and died on the cross, expecting nothing in return. He was the sinless one, but he suffered as only the worst of us might perhaps deserve to suffer. It was not fair. That is true—and the good and the evil alike received the benefit, just as in so many gospel stories—the prodigal son was better treated than the well-behaved, loyal, elder son (Luke 15:11–32); the publicans and sinners, tax collectors and prostitutes were favored over the law-abiding Pharisees (Luke 7:29–30). All receive God's benefits and love. He has loved us first. He gave all to us; so we too, to the extent that we believe in him, make his standard ours. We too want to be kind to the ungrateful and the selfish. Anyone can be kind to those who are pleasantly grateful and loving. Anyone can be generous to others who show themselves generous or deserving. But we are to practice the mercy of Christ: "Judge not and you will

58 : The Season of the Year

not be judged. . . . Be merciful even as your Father is merciful."

In 1998 this is the last Sunday before Lent. For the readings of the next and following Sundays in that year, turn to the Lenten series.

Eighth Sunday of the Year

Reading 1: Sirach 27:4–7

Responsorial: Psalm 92:1–2, 12–13, 14–15

Reading 2: 1 Corinthians 15:54–58

Gospel: Luke 6:39–45

one Lord, Jesus Christ
for us and for our salvation
for our sake . . . crucified

Today's gospel completes the Great Sermon in Luke's gospel. The point of these closing lines of the sermon is to be sure that we personally apply everything Jesus has said: I to myself and you to yourself, in your own heart alone. The sermon contained, you remember, such disturbing principles as love your enemies; do good to those who hate you, turn the other cheek, give to everyone who asks of you, do not try to recover what others take from you; in fact, give them more than they took, forgive everyone everything; judge no one; condemn no one. The reason behind them is that they express in different ways the very central pattern of our faith: this is the way God has treated us; this is the way Christ has lived and died for us.

Of course we squirm when we hear these things, because they are hardly an accurate picture of the way we live our daily lives. So we twist about and look for ways of escape. He cannot mean that! Yet the words are so clear. Or he is talking about someone else! But no one else does these things, why should I? (Although Christ did not say, "But no one else is going to be crucified; why should I?")

So the conclusion of the sermon tries to make sure we apply all this to ourselves, each one alone in his or her own heart. Do not apply them to others at all, or worry about others, or use them to make yourself a *teacher,* but set yourself to practice them personally. How could you be a teacher of them when you have not yet penetrated their meaning in your personal practice? "Can the blind lead the blind? Will they not both fall into a pit?" (Luke 6:39).

Do not turn to examine your brother or sister: "Why do you see the speck that is in your brother's eye, but do not notice your own eye has a log sticking out of it?" So you want to say, "Let's have everybody else forgive me and then I'll start forgiving everyone else. Let's have people hand me their goods freely and for nothing, then perhaps I could give away my own. Let people stop criticizing me, then I'll be happy to love them without judgment." But no. You cannot say, "Brother, let me take out the speck that is in your eye," so long as you yourself do not have a clear eye: "You hypocrite," says Jesus; "first take the log out of your own eye, and then you will see clearly to take out the speck that is in your brother's eye."

The point of the teachings of this sermon is to grasp really and fully what we say we believe when we recite, he "suffered, died and was buried . . . rose again . . . ascended into heaven"—and all this "for our sake. . . . for us and for our salvation." What this really means is that our salvation is that which happened to Christ, and nothing else. There is no salvation except in being willing to give ourselves as he gave himself, to forgive as he has forgiven us, to love as he has loved us, to be ready to suffer and die in trust in God our Father rather than bring pain on any human being, to let the full weight of the sin of this world fall on us and not grumble at it, but love and forgive and perhaps die in the process, because we know that God judges justly and is working out our good and our happiness in whatever he allows to happen.

To understand this is to understand our Christian faith, professed in our Creed. The Creed is not just a collection of stories, a mythological hodgepodge of divine interventions, a savior-god "zooming in" to perform wonders and make the world gape. It is a statement of how we are saved by our full trust in God, in the midst of all the horrible things that sin can bring upon us; it is a statement of faith in how God's love coming to us in Christ and the Spirit which fills his church, can transform sickness into health, suffering into joy, death into life.

This Great Sermon illuminates that for us, makes it more concrete. It is a concise application of our Creed in practice, just as the Creed itself is meant to be a short summary of the gospel as a whole. At the end of the sermon Jesus warns us that this is the test of our faith. Do we say in the Creed, "We believe?" Then ask yourself for once seriously what that means. You believe . . . ? Check yourself: "For no good tree bears bad fruit, nor again does a bad tree bear good fruit. Each tree is known by its own fruit. The good man produces good; the evil man produces evil." You believe? Then how about your own life—no one else's. No one but you can answer for your life. To what extent do you live by the pattern of Christ revealed in the Creed, explained in practical detail in this sermon? What kind of person are you? "Figs are not gathered from thorns, nor are grapes picked from a bramble bush." If you are a Christian, is the fruit that comes forth in your own life the fruit of works in the Christian pattern Christ has here held up to us?

In a further sentence of this sermon, not quoted for us in today's reading, Jesus adds to the above, "Why do you call me Lord, Lord, and not do what I tell you?" (Luke 6:46). That can be our thought for the week. We can take it home with us, turn it over in our mind. We have read the Great Sermon. We know what it is to be a Christian: Not just saying, "Lord, Lord," but loving and giving and forgiving and being ready to suffer and die as he did. In the Creed we say, "We believe in one Lord, Jesus Christ." He asks, "Why do you call me Lord, Lord, and not do what I tell you?" What is our answer?

In 1992 and 1995, this is the last Sunday before Lent.

First Sunday of Lent

Reading 1: Deuteronomy 26:4–10

Responsorial: Psalm 91:1–2, 10–11, 14–15

Reading 2: Romans 10:8–13

Gospel: Luke 4:1–13

We believe in one God,
   the Father, the Almighty
   maker of heaven and earth,
   of all that is seen and unseen.

The reading from Deuteronomy describes a ceremony which the people of Israel were to perform when first they came into the promised land. As soon as they had raised their first crops, they were to come to the altar of the Lord with a basketful of the best of the first-fruits of that crop. The priest was to take the basket from them, put it before the altar of God, and then they were to rehearse before God the story of all the good things God had given them and had done for them, since the time of Abraham, their first father. Abraham had begun as a lonely, poor, wandering exile, his descendants had fallen into slavery in Egypt, but God had freed them and made them into a great people with a land of their own, loading them with prosperity, health, and every other blessing.

All this happened by God's good will and free choice. God had heard their prayers and brought them into this land flowing with milk and honey. Therefore they were to bring the first-fruit of the ground, "which thou, O Lord, hast given me." They were to "set it down before the Lord your God, and worship before the Lord your God."

Our Creed too begins, "We believe in God, the Father almighty, Maker of heaven and earth, of all that is seen and unseen." This is our confession that everything we have comes from God. He did not just own the earth we live on and then give it to us. He made the earth. He made the stars. He made us. We believe in him far more completely than we believe in anybody or anything else.

We are happy to remind ourselves of how much he has done for us. Like the Creed, the ordinary blessing or grace at table is a recognition of how our daily life comes to us as part of God's work of creation. There is nothing in the world that is not in God's hand; nothing that does not owe its entire existence to him.

So in the temptation stories in today's gospel, Christ's ultimate answer to the devil's temptations is to recall from whom all these things come, to whom then they really belong, and under whose control they are. The devil would tempt Christ to use his power for himself, feeding himself miraculously, floating down from the top tower of the temple, grasping the power and the glory of all the governments of this world. The devil claims that "it has been delivered to me, and I give it to whom I will . . . worship me and it shall all be yours." But the answer ultimately is, "You shall worship the Lord your God, and him only shall you serve." He is the creator, owner, and master of it all: "You shall not tempt the Lord your God."

In the gospel story the devil falsely says the kingdoms of this earth belong to him. In a sense they do, insofar as they surrender themselves to his way of thinking and acting. But the Creed says God is "Maker . . . of all that is seen and unseen," and that means that ultimately even the devil owes his existence to God. Not that God ever created an evil being, but God could create spiritual beings with an intelligence like ours or better. Such beings would have the same personal freedom you and I do—freedom to choose to do good or evil. If they did choose evil, they would be perverting their own nature, just as we pervert ours when we yield to selfishness and sin. They would be making themselves into devils from angels, just as we can change ourselves from children of God to children of the devil.

In tempting Jesus, the devil quotes the Scripture (for, as we say, "even the devil can quote Scripture to his own purposes"). He cites the text, "He will give his angels charge of you, lest you strike your foot against a stone." The first part of that quotation occurs in the psalm for today, which tells how God protects those who trust in him and believe in him: "No evil shall befall you, no scourge come near your tent, for he will give his angels charge of you to guard you in all your ways. . . When he calls to me, I will answer him, I will be with him in trouble, I will rescue him and honor him." These lines apply to everyone who "dwells in the shelter of the Most High, who abides in the shadow of the Almighty." For God, our creator and Father, is "my refuge and my fortress; my God, in whom I trust."

This is the God of the Creed: Father of all, maker of all; Father to all he has made. From him comes every blessing, and from him all fatherhood in heaven and on earth draws its name. We recall all this on this first Sunday of Lent because, as the prayer for today puts it, You, Lord God, creator and Father, "formed man from the clay of the earth and breathed into him the breath of life; but he turned from your face and sinned. In this time of repentance we call out for your mercy." When God created human beings, the Bible says God put before them all the animals, all the fruits of the earth. These were to belong to us and be enjoyed by us. But sin has changed that happy, planned relationship of humankind to the world. Because of sin we find we work in the world with difficulty and suffering. Lent is the time to repent of the sins which have been our own contribution to the difficulties of the human race. It is a time to return to God our creator as to the Father that he really is, acknowledging that all comes from his goodness; asking to be restored to the fullness of his love.

Second Sunday of Lent

Reading 1: Genesis 15:5–12, 17–18

Responsorial: Psalm 27:1, 7–8a, 8bc–9abc, 13–14

Reading 2: Philippians 3:17–4:1

Gospel: Luke 9:28–36

God, the Father, the Almighty,
maker of heaven and earth

The absolute dominion of God as creator of all is shown again in the selection from Genesis. God, who made heaven and earth and all that is in them, can obviously dispose of them as he pleases. In today's selection he has Abram look at the stars of heaven, and promises to Abram descendants equal in number to the stars. He has Abram bring him five different animals for sacrifice, as a sign of his universal dominion. Over that solemn sacrifice, God promises Abram and his descendants all the land that lay before him "from the river of Egypt to the great river, the river Euphrates."

This is the one true God, whom all nations and individuals must confess. As the passge from Phillipians tells us, people search out other gods for themselves: for some "their god is the belly"; they keep their "minds set on earthly things." These are "enemies of the cross of Christ." But the God who created heaven and earth, the seen and the unseen, wants us to remember that our commonwealth is ultimately in heaven. He wants us to live by faith, that as the body Jesus surrendered to death became a glorious body, so he "will change our lowly body to be like his."

In the meantime, it is up to us to hear the words which Jesus has left us; to believe him when he tells us the way to God. And that is the point of the great manifestation of God the Father in today's gospel. There, while Jesus is praying, we see his body transformed into what it will be later in glory. Over those who are watching, there passes a great cloud of glory—a traditional sign of the presence of God. From that cloud they hear the voice of the Father: "This is my Son, my Chosen. Listen to him!"

God the Father does not often manifest himself directly. In the gospel he speaks at Jesus' baptism, here, and perhaps one other time (John 12:28f.). That is because we are to know God from knowing Jesus, who is God's Word made flesh: "No one had ever seen God; the only-begotten Son who is in the bosom of the Father, he has revealed him."

This is the theme of the prayer for today's mass, which says, "Father of light, in you is found no shadow of change." This is a citation from the letter of James: "Every good endowment and every perfect gift is from above, coming down from the Father of lights, with whom there is no variation or shadow due to change (James 1:17). This is the God described in 1 Timothy as "the blessed and only Sovereign, the King of kings and Lord of lords, who alone has immortality and dwells in unapproachable light, whom no man has ever seen or can see" (1 Timothy 6:15f.).

The prayer of today's mass ties in this notion of God with our lenten efforts at repentance and renewal: "Father of light, in whom is found no shadow of change, but only the fullness of life and limitless truth. Open our hearts to the voice of your Word"—that is, of Jesus Christ, the Word incarnate—"and free us from the original darkness that shadows our vision. Restore our sight that we may look upon your Son, who calls us to repentance and to a change of heart, for he lives and reigns with you for ever and ever."

Finally, we appeal to the Father, the "maker of heaven and earth," in the blessing of today's mass: "Lord, we rejoice that you are our Creator and Ruler. As we call upon your generosity, renew and keep us in your love."

Third Sunday of Lent

Reading 1: Exodus 3:1–8a, 13–15
Responsorial: Psalm 103:1–2, 3–4, 6–7, 8, 11
Reading 2: 1 Corinthians 10:1–6, 10–12
Gospel: Luke 13:1–9

*God, the Father, the Almighty,
maker of heaven and earth*

    God the Father, first Person of the blessed Trinity, is known to us really only insofar as we come to know Jesus Christ, his Son. We say, "God, the Father almighty, Maker of heaven and earth," but it is no less true that the Son is almighty and is equally maker of heaven and earth. That is, the God of the Old Testament, the God people knew before Christ came, was always the one true God, Father, Son, and Holy Spirit, just as God is Father, Son, and Holy Spirit today. But before Christ came, God was not *known* as Father, Son, and Holy Spirit. God was simply God. Human beings could know of God's inner life only what God chose to reveal: That has never been very much.
    One of the most important revelations of God in the Old Testament was God's description of himself to Moses. In answer to the question, "What is your name?" God said: "I AM WHO I AM. Say this to the people of Israel: 'I AM has sent me to you.' " This is God as known before Jesus: "I AM," "I AM WHO I AM." But that is just a statement of reality—of exis-

tence—of fact. God is the ultimate given; God is the absolute that simply is always there, no matter how much other things may come and go. God can always be relied on: he is always there. He is the fountain of being. He is the meaning of all existence. He is the fullness for which all existence strives.

This same name appears once in the New Testament, in the powerful scene where Jesus compares himself to the patriarch Abraham, and says, "Before Abraham was, I am" (John 8:58)—I AM. Reality. Being. It is a fitting name for the one true God. Yet this name does not seem to give us much information about what God is like. It simply tells us directly that God is always there. We understand correctly that it also implies God is always there when we need him: he will always be there *for us*.

God revealed himself in the Old Testament as a God of forgiveness, patience, love. Look at the psalm for today, for instance, with its refrain, "The Lord is kind and merciful."

> The Lord is merciful and gracious, slow to anger and abounding in steadfast love. As the heavens are high above the earth, so great is his steadfast love toward those who fear him. The Lord is kind and merciful."

Such thoughts run through much of the Bible. So do other thoughts—of God's jealousy, anger, vengeance. Even Paul appeals to those and so does Jesus. Paul writes in the letter to the Corinthians that the calamities of many of the people in the wilderness "happened to them as a warning but they were written down for our instruction . . . so that one who thinks that he stands take heed lest he fall." And Jesus, in today's gospel, refers to some apparent accidents that have happened, and to some persecutions, then adds, "Unless you repent, you will all likewise perish."

Behind these statements lies the knowledge also of God as the great controller of the universe. He watches over all that happens; he takes care of us in love; he will also, when we need it, as children, chastise us in order to bring us to repentance. The events of life are not haphazard. They do not happen to us without the knowledge and consent of God. This is called his providence, and it follows from the fact that God is creator. For everything is his creation. Therefore everything that comes to us should be received by us as coming from his hand. He has made us free and intelligent creatures—we are also constantly being called upon by him to make the future better, to correct faults, to relieve suffering, insofar as it lies in our power. God's providence is not an excuse for us to be passive and let the future take care of itself, for God's providence works only through us. But when we have done the best we can—and even when we have not—then, when the result actually occurs, when the reality is there, we must understand that it is God's reality. The obvious good in it is his good and for our good. Its obvious or apparent evil is only a further challenge to us, an obstacle to be overcome, a flaw to be reworked later and finally into a larger good. But we always trust in him, and live in confidence in his love.

Fourth Sunday of Lent

Reading 1: Joshua 5:9, 10–12

Responsorial: Psalm 34:1–2, 3–4, 5–6

Reading 2: 2 Corinthians 5:17–21

Gospel: Luke 15:1–3, 11–32

the forgiveness of sins

The theme of today's mass is joy: "Rejoice Jerusalem! Be glad for her, those who love her; rejoice with her those of you who mourned for her." This is another "rejoicing Sunday," coming in the middle of Lent, as the first one came in the middle of Advent. The reason for today's rejoicing is the commemoration of the most joyful article of our Creed: "the forgiveness of sins."

In the Creed, the forgiveness of sins is linked with baptism: "We acknowledge one baptism for the remission of sins." But the forgiveness of sins which comes to us with baptism can be renewed in our lives whenever it is needed; that is, whenever we fall into sin. When that renewal takes place, whether through the sacrament of reconciliation or through private repentance, it is always the same marvelous phenomenon which is at the heart of Christianity: God's love is always ready and able to embrace us and transform us. Our baptism put the mark of his forgiveness upon us; not so that we might go out and sin freely ("God forbid!" says St. Paul [Romans 6:15]), but that we might live in love, and be ready to extend the same forgiveness to others who have injured us. There is no better, no more rapid and secure road to a happy, human society in this world, than reflecting on the forgiving love of God.

Nevertheless, the simple reality is that we do sometimes fail and fall along the way; so part of the message of our Christian baptism is that when we do fail, all is not lost. God never abandons us: "He who did not spare his own Son, but has given him up for us all, will he not also give us all things together with him? (Romans 8:32).

So Paul says, in 2 Corinthians, that, beginning with baptism, if anyone is in Christ, he is a new creation: "The old has passed away, behold the new is come." This is the baptismal message: "God, through Christ, has reconciled us to himself." Our baptism recalls and reactivates in us the reality which God's Son performed "for us and for our salvation." But from that reality and from that one moment of our baptism grows, says Paul, a whole "ministry of reconciliation." "There is entrusted to us the message of reconciliation." And if anyone in Christ falls into sin, "God makes his appeal through us: we beseech you on behalf of Christ, be reconciled to God." The way to forgiveness always stands open.

That way is explained for us more fully in the gospel story of the prodigal son. The younger son wastes the inheritance he has from his father and finally debases himself, ruins his life, until the very wretchedness of his state drives him to self-awareness. He must arise and go to his father and confess: "Father, I have sinned; I am no longer worthy to be called your son."

But as soon as the young man begins to act on this realization, he finds to his surprise that his father is ready and waiting for him; he has been wanting to love and forgive him, is eager to restore him to the fullness of his previous life as a beloved son.

That is what God is like. That is the forgiveness always ready for us when we need it. And that gives us plenty over which to rejoice today.

Only one thing can spoil the rejoicing. What if we ourselves do not share the same sentiments as God? What if we are not ready to extend forgiveness to others, as we hope to be forgiven by God? What if we cling to the feeling that justice should prevail over mercy?

Then the joy of the Christian message can soon be spoiled. Then we are not like God, like the father in the story, but rather like the elder son. Then the joy of this day can be spoiled, for that means we hold ourselves back from the heavenly rejoicing. If we continue in such sentiments, we can hold ourselves back from the heavenly rejoicing and the joys of the heavenly banquet forever: for the Christian must be able to say without hesitation and without grudge, "We acknowledge one baptism for the forgiveness of sins."

The prayers for today's mass help make clear this meaning in the forgiveness we have received through Christ:

> We are joyful in your Word, who reconciles us to you. (He) spoke peace to a sinful world, and brought mankind the gift of reconciliation by the suffering and death he endured. Teach us, the people who bear his name, to follow the example he gave us: may our faith, hope and charity turn hatred to love, conflict to peace, death to eternal life.

Fifth Sunday of Lent

Reading 1: Isaiah 43:16–21

Responsorial: Psalm 126:1–2ab, 2cd–3, 4–5, 6

Reading 2: Philippians 3:8–14

Gospel: John 8:1–11

For us and for our salvation . . . for our sake
the forgiveness of sins
the life of the world to come

    We are drawing near the end of Lent. The theme of conversion from sin, repentance, forgiveness, continues, always looking to the great motive and cause of our reconciliation and forgiveness—the passion, death, and resurrection of Christ our Lord.

    So today's gospel is the gospel of the forgiveness of the woman caught in the act of adultery. When Jesus says to her, "Neither do I condemn you; go and do not sin again," he speaks God's forgiveness, God's perfect willingness to accept any sinner. But in the same gospel, by the way he acts toward the persons who brought the woman before him, he underlines again the need that God's forgiveness be spread abroad in this world by our human readiness to forgive one another.

    Faced with his challenge, "Let him who is without sin among you be the first to throw a stone at her," the bystanders all went away, one by one, beginning with the eldest. Why? Because among all those people, even as among all in the church today, there was no one without sin—not one: "Let him who is without sin among you be the first to throw a stone." Not one of us could face that challenge, if Christ laid it down before us this day.

That means that each and every one of us has need of forgiveness, and so again we must "acknowledge one baptism for the forgiveness of sins." And we must all look with gratitude to what God did, sending his Son "for us and for our salvation." For our sake "he was crucified under Pontius Pilate, suffered, died and was buried." And it was for our sake that "on the third day he rose again in fulfillment of the Scriptures." For our sake "he ascended into heaven and is seated at the right hand of the Father." And for our sake, too, "he will come again in glory to judge the living and the dead."

Therefore Paul reminds us in the reading from Philippians, "I count everything as loss because of the surpassing worth of knowing Christ Jesus my Lord." What Paul says he wants above all is "that I may know him and the power of his resurrection, and may share his sufferings."

This is what the season of Lent is about, that by "sharing in his sufferings," we may "become like him in his death, that if possible we may attain the resurrection from the dead." Through the sufferings of this life, through the sacrifices of Lent, through union with Christ's passion and death, we hope to attain the joys of Easter—not because we have earned them, but because God in Christ has given them to us. If we learn to "count everything as loss because of the surpassing worth of knowing Christ Jesus"; if "for his sake we suffer the loss of all things and count them as refuse in order that we may gain Christ and be found in him," it is that we may be made fit to receive God's greatest gift: full union with him in the Holy Spirit.

Salvation is finally a gift of God, not something we attain by ourselves and for ourselves. But God never refuses that gift to those who open themselves to it generously. God gives that gift to those who, with Paul, press on to make it my own, because Christ Jesus has made me his own. I do not consider that I have made it my own: but one thing I do, forgetting what lies behind and straining forward to what lies ahead, I press on toward the goal for the prize of the upward call of God in Christ Jesus.

That, to return to the gospel, is what Jesus invites the woman to do: to forget what lies behind, to turn her eyes completely to what lies ahead: " 'Has anyone condemned you?' 'No one, Lord.' 'Neither do I condemn you. Go and sin no more.' " And that, of course, is his invitation to us.

As the Isaiah passage says, "Remember not the former things nor consider the things of old. Behold, I am doing a new thing, now it springs forth, do you not perceive it?" We advance toward the last days of Lent in the spirit of opening ourselves to this new thing, ready to join Christ in his sufferings and death "for us and for our salvation . . . for our sake . . . for the forgiveness of sins."

Passion Sunday (Palm Sunday)

Gospel for the Procession: Luke 19:28–40

Reading 1: Isaiah 50:4–7

Responsorial: Psalm 22:7–8, 16–17a, 18–19, 22–23ab

Reading 2: Philippians 2:6–11

Gospel: Luke 22:14–23:56

eternally begotten of the Father,
God from God, Light from Light,
true God from true God . . .
one in Being with the Father . . .
For us and for our salvation
he came down from heaven . . . and became man.
For our sake he was crucified . . . suffered,
died . . . buried . . . rose . . . ascended . . .
is seated at the right hand of the Father . . .
will come again in glory . . .
and his kingdom will have no end.

Today's readings and prayers focus on the heart of our Christian faith: the saving value of Jesus' voluntary self-surrender in obedience and love to suffering and death for our sake. They are practically self-explanatory, and, since they include the entire passion narrative, they are long. So let us here be brief.

The reading from Isaiah stresses the voluntary self-surrender of God's servant in utter trust and obedience to God: "The

Lord God has opened my ear; and I was not rebellious. I turned not backward: I gave my back to the smiters and my cheeks to those who pulled out my beard; I hid not my face from shame and spitting."

The psalm is that quoted so aptly in the passion narrative itself:

> "My God, my God, why have you abandoned me? All who see me mock at me, they make mouths at me, they wag their heads: He committed his cause to the Lord, let him deliver him, let him rescue him for he delights in him. . . . They have pierced my hands and feet; I can count all my bones. They divided my garments among them, and for my raiment they cast lots.

All these lines are familiar to us from the story of Christ's sufferings. The writers of the gospels used these very lines from the ancient psalm in order to tell the story of the passion in such a way as to make clear that it all happened according to the intention and plan of God ("in fulfillment of the Scriptures").

Paul, to the Philippians, states the whole doctrine, almost exactly as we find it in the Creed we say at mass every Sunday. He writes that Christ Jesus, "though he was in the form of God, did not count equality with God a thing to be grasped, but emptied himself, taking the form of a servant, being born in the likeness of men." We express this when we confess that Jesus Christ was "eternally begotten of the Father, God from God, Light from Light, true God from true God," and that he "for us and for our salvation came down from heaven . . . and became man."

Then Paul continues, "and being found in human form, he humbled himself and became obedient unto death, even death on a cross." In the Creed we say, "For our sake he was crucified under Pontius Pilate, suffered, died and was buried." Paul writes further that "Therefore God has highly exalted him and bestowed on him the name which is above every name." So we confess: "On the third day he rose again . . . he ascended into heaven and is seated at the right hand of the Father."

Finally, Paul's hymn concludes, "That at the name of Jesus every knee should bow, in heaven and on earth and under the earth, and every tongue confess that Jesus Christ is Lord." So in the Creed we say, "He will come again in glory to judge the living and the dead. And his kingdom will have no end."

There follows the entire text of the passion of our Lord according to Luke. We listen to it as the story of our salvation.

Holy Thursday

Reading 1: Exodus 12:1–8, 11–14
Responsorial: Psalm 116:12–13, 15, 16bc, 17–18
Reading 2: 1 Corinthians 11:23–26
Gospel: John 13:1–15

We believe

The readings for today recall the principal points which this day itself exists to commemorate. The Exodus text prescribes the killing and eating of the Passover lamb, and the use of its blood as a sign marking the houses to be spared when destruction and death came to the land of Egypt. We read this passage today because Jesus ate the Passover meal with his disciples before himself going out to suffer and die as the true lamb of God who takes away the sins of the world; and because on this day he told us to continue the sacred community meal in his memory until he comes again.

The passage from 1 Corinthians describes Jesus' actions the night before he died: his presenting us with the bread—his body—and the cup—the new covenant in his blood, which we are to drink in remembrance of him, to proclaim "the Lord's death until he comes." The meaning of the Eucharist for Paul includes the recollection of what Jesus has done for us in suffering, dying, and rising; it also includes a looking forward to his coming again. Thus the realities which the Eucharist exists to commemorate and to make present to us are the realities spoken of in the Creed.

The gospel according to John shows the great love for us which Jesus felt that last night, and reminds us how all he did was done "for us and for our salvation." He knew the death that awaited him, but he went toward it and into it surely, relentlessly. Then, by a special gesture at the supper, he invited his disciples, and us as well, to join him on that road of suffering and death leading to resurrection glory.

This was the gesture of the foot-washing. It was, he tells us, an example: "If I then, your Lord and Teacher, have washed your feet, you also ought to wash one another's feet. For I have given you an example, that you also should do as I have done to you." But the foot-washing was not only an example to be mechanically imitated. It was itself a powerful symbol which could effectively proclaim so much of Jesus' message. The foot-washing stands for the humility which astounded the disciples—as we see in Peter's protest "You shall never wash my feet." It stands for Christ's great love, described in the opening lines: "having loved his own who were in the world, he loved them to the end." It stands for service: as Luke's gospel tells us how Jesus said at that same last meal, "I am in your midst as the one who serves" (Luke 22:27).

All these meanings have implications for Christian living: "Learn of me, for I am gentle and lowly of heart" (Matthew 11:29); "Love one another as I have loved you" (John 15:12); "Whoever would be great among you must be your servant, and whoever would be first among you must be the slave of all" (Mark 10:43f.); "I have given you an example, that you also should do as I have done to you"; "He has laid down his life for us; we also should lay down our lives for the brethren" (1 John 3:16).

All these things are part of the meaning of that last meal together, which became our Christian Eucharist. All these things are part of the meaning of Jesus' suffering and dying "for us and for our salvation." When we say "for our sake he was crucified," this is what the words mean, and this should be the pattern of our lives. Our belief is not just a matter of taking, on someone else's word, a collection of historical facts we could have discovered for ourselves by careful investigation. For us, believing implies appreciating the meaning of these facts and accepting them with all their implications, even though the truth of these implications could never be proved by anyone's investigation or by any argument of reason alone.

We only know Christ died for us because that is the faith which we have received from the church, and which we recognize as a message from God. Only in the same way can we know that what Christ did had value for us and for our salvation. We only know that Jesus will come again in glory because we believe this message. And we only know that it is better to serve than to be served, that it is God's wish we love one another unto death and be ready to lay down anything, even our very lives, for the sake of others, because that is taught us as God's word and recognized by us in faith as the kind of word our loving God would speak. So we know only by faith that this bread and wine we share are Christ's own body and blood given for us and able to transform us into him. So with good reason this faith is to us the gift of God precious beyond all others. It is the very key to life itself.

Good Friday

Reading 1: Isaiah 52:13–53:12

Responsorial: Psalm 31:1, 5, 11–12, 14–15, 16, 24

Reading 2: Hebrews 4:14–16; 5:7–9

Gospel: John 18:1–19:42

We believe . . . for us

Today we meditate on the fact that God is truly dead. He died for us on Calvary, after terrible suffering. The liturgy of today gives an adequate reflection on this theme, particularly the passion story itself as told by Saint John. The reading from Isaiah describes how the just one, who had no sin, surrendered himself to death: "wounded for our transgressions, bruised for our iniquities; upon him was the chastisement that made us whole, and with his stripes we are healed."

Isaiah in those words is describing his vision of the role of the just throughout history, especially the just people of Israel. Their willingness to bear the injustices heaped upon them, their readiness to trust in the Lord in spite of all and to continue to love and serve their fellows, constitutes the hope of the world. If each one of us demanded justice be done us, was always balancing the scales, giving tit for tat, repaying whatever evil anyone did to us, shoving ahead, trying to get his or her share "before the greedy people take it all," the world would—well, the world would go on just as it has been going on, just as the sad mess it is today.

But God proposes a different way, the way which Jesus takes and along which he leads. In Jesus' way, the sins of all the world do take their natural horrible effect—until the one person who knows himself without guilt personally says finally, "the buck stops here!" No returning of evil for evil, but from now on, only good for evil. So "he was oppressed, and he was afflicted, yet he opened not his mouth; like a lamb that is led to the slaughter, and like a sheep that before its shearers is dumb, so he opened not his mouth. By oppression and judgment he was taken away," but—the prophet makes clear—this precisely will be his triumph, his victory. This will be his and our salvation.

In the passion story according to John, we see the many ironies. Above all we see how Jesus' final failure in death by torture is his hour of glory to which all his life has been moving. It is his return to the Father, as the seed falling into the ground dies, and brings forth much fruit. The passage from Hebrews sums this up by saying that Jesus "learned obedience through what he suffered; and being made perfect he became the source of eternal salvation to all who obey him."

There is here a level of mystery that shall never be captured in words and reasons. The Christian faith from the beginning has been that Jesus died for our sins. No one has ever provided a logically compelling reason why he really had to do so, nor formulated any philosophically satisfying account of just why his dying should have had any effect on actions we had committed, guilt we had incurred. Many explanations have been offered, but none really makes complete good sense. Finally, it seems that the reason the Scripture does not tell us this is because there is no need for us to know it. The simple fact is more impressive and more expressive than any theoretical account of it could be. The fact is, moreover, so rich that it can give rise to many different theoretical accounts.

What matters however, is the personal confrontation implied in the message about that fact. "He loved me," Paul wrote, "and delivered himself for me" (Galatians 2:20), though Jesus in his lifetime had never laid eyes on Paul, nor Paul on Jesus. How then could Paul think that Jesus had loved him personally and died for him? He could believe this, as we can, because he believed that in Christ the ancient prophecy had been fulfilled: "God himself will come and save you" (Isaiah 35:4). For this we are grateful, and stand in awe, appreciative of what love can be; appreciative of what God's love is, and of the horrible effects of sin, whether or not we can begin to understand all this.

Easter Vigil

Epistle: Romans 6:3–11

Responsorial: Psalm 118:1–2, 15–16a, 17, 22–23

Gospel: Luke 24:1–12

Easter Day

Reading 1: Acts 10:34a, 37–43

Responsorial: Psalm 118:1–2, 15–16a, 17, 22–23

Reading 2: Colossians 3:1–4
　　or 1 Corinthians 5:6b–8

Gospel: John 20:1–9
　　or (for an afternoon mass) Luke 24:13–35

On the third day he rose again
in fulfillment of the Scriptures

　　We celebrate Christ's resurrection not just as we might celebrate the return of a good friend or a loved and admired hero. We celebrate especially because it is "the fulfillment of the

Scriptures." What does that mean, "the fulfillment of the Scriptures"?

It refers above all to the fact that the Scriptures—the whole Old Testament—are full of promises. The vigil readings give us some of these. Beginning with the creation story on the first pages of Genesis, the story of God's people is a story of promises and threats from God, as well as a series of partial fulfillments of those promises and threats. No matter what disaster threatened or occurred, God was going to save. No matter how flourishing the people, their continued happiness and prosperity was linked to continuing loyalty to him.

As history developed, sometimes these promises seemed to come true, sometimes they seemed not to. Or sometimes they seemed fulfilled in part, but only in part, with much left for the future. Still, the absolute quality of the promises remained: "No matter what happens to you, I will be with you to save you." For those who wished to take seriously these divine assurances, it became necessary to reflect on the history and ask questions. And they also could not help but ask reflective questions concerning the promises themselves. For instance, how far did God intend them to go? Did God mean his assurances to be absolute and ultimate? What about the extreme instance of what could happen? What if we are killed? What then? Does God's promise of care for us extend even to that point—and beyond?

In Christ, God's promise of safekeeping was fulfilled in a way that showed it was an absolute promise and ultimate. Christ died an outcast, a criminal, a failure, an apparent fraud—one who had appealed to God's great plans and promises, but had not been protected by God in his own necessity. The resurrection of Christ was the answer to the promises: God *is* there to save; and he can do it, even in the extreme. And he will do it; he does it; he has in fact done it. And he will do it for *us*.

This is so true and so real for Saint Paul that he writes in the letter to the Colossians (the second reading for Easter day) that we have *already* risen with Christ. We have died with him and been raised with him; now we should live as people who have been raised from the dead, with our minds on things above, not on those things that are on earth.

How have we already truly died and risen with Christ? Paul explains it in the second reading for the vigil mass (Romans 6:3–11). He refers to the reality of our baptism. Our baptism was not just an external gesture performed upon us. It was a pledge taken in our name. It was a response, made in our name, to the good news of Christ's death and resurrection. In our baptism we were marked with the sign of Christ's cross. The pattern of salvation through cross and resurrection became *our* pattern. We were made Christians by baptism because we were made other Christs, joyously accepting the gospel of cross/resurrection as good news *for us*, as *our* good news, to be lived out in *our* own lives.

For that reason, it does not suffice to think of Christ's death for us and be sorry for our sins that caused it. It does not suffice to be observers of the laws and commandments. It does not suffice just to believe in the promises. We are called to believe *this* promise—that God will save us even from final suffering and death; to live now as persons who have indeed accepted death with Christ, and been already gifted with new life in him.

Note the prayer of the Easter mass: "This is the morning on which the Lord appeared to men who had begun to lose hope, and opened their eyes to what the Scriptures foretold: that first he must die, and then he would rise and ascend into his Father's glorious presence." And note the introduction to the baptismal promises to be renewed today: "Through the paschal mystery, we have been buried in Christ in baptism so that we may rise with him to a new life."

Second Sunday of Easter

Reading 1: Acts 5:12–16

Responsorial: Psalm 118:2–4, 22–24, 25–27ab

Reading 2: Revelation 1:9–11a, 12–13, 17–19

Gospel: John 20:19–31

one . . . apostolic Church

the forgiveness of sins

Today is the second Sunday of Easter. The celebration of Easter lasts nine weeks, through seven Sundays of Easter, then Pentecost, and Trinity Sunday. During this period the general theme will be the continuation of the spirit of Easter, "a spirit of joyful faith and of confident hope" (*Lectionary*). We said last Sunday that as Christians we are to live new lives, as if risen with Christ. The readings of these Sundays of Easter will help show us how this is done, what these new and risen lives should be like.

For this, the first several gospel selections will show some of the appearances of the risen Lord; then there will follow passages from our Lord's last instructions to his disciples, given at the last supper, the night before he died. The first readings through this time will come not, as usual, from the Old Testament, but from the Acts of the Apostles. The Acts of the Apostles is written by the author of the gospel of Luke, the gospel we have been studying this year. The Acts tells the story of what happened to Jesus' disciples after his resurrection and ascension. It is the story of the earliest years of the Christian community Jesus left behind him. It is the story of the beginnings of the church, and all through the Easter season it will enable us to see how the first disciples began to live their transformed, risen lives in Christ.

Finally, the second readings for the Sundays of Easter will be taken from the book of Revelation, sometimes called the Apocalypse. "Apocalypse" is the Greek word for "revelation." This is the last book of the New Testament and the last book of the Bible. It is the account of a vision of its author, John, in which he has a revelation of Christ and the saints in glory. Thus it gives us a picture of what is meant by "the risen life." It gives a focus to our thoughts when we try to follow the Easter injunction, "set your mind on the things above, where Christ is seated at the right hand of God." At the same time, the Revelation of John is also a picture of the struggles which the Christian community must undergo on the road to final glory. It concludes with a description of God's final salvation and happiness for all who are saved.

Today's first reading is a picture of the early growth in numbers of the Christian community in Jerusalem. The gift of healing as exercised by the apostles, and especially by Peter, played a large role in many early conversions. The Christian message of life and deliverance was also always a message of healing from afflictions and illness. The gift of life in Christ overflowed into all aspects, all corners, of life.

The second reading begins our reading of the book of Revelation, and begins with the vision of the risen Christ himself and of his description of himself: "I am the living one. I died, and behold, I am alive for evermore, and I have the keys of Death and Hades." He died and now lives—this is what makes him the Christ, the Savior.

The gospel shows the beginnings of the new Christian community, when Jesus appears to the disciples for the first time. It is Easter Sunday evening. Jesus speaks to the disciples: "Peace be with you. As the Father has sent me, even so I send you." And, breathing on them, he says, "Receive the Holy Spirit. If you forgive the sins of any, they are forgiven; if you retain the sins of any, they are retained."

So the first step in the risen life of the new community is receiving a share in Christ's risen life. The new and risen life is a life in Christ's Holy Spirit. He gives it to the twelve, who will pass it to others. It is a life of forgiveness first of all: notice that the promised forgiveness of sins will take place through the disciples themselves. They are told that those whose sins they forgive will be forgiven. Those sins they retain will be retained. Frequently people object to the ancient practice of confession: "I confess my sins only to God, because only from God do I ask forgiveness." We do confess to God and expect our forgiveness from him. But Christ says here clearly that his forgiveness will come to us through those on whom he has breathed the Holy Spirit.

The church begins also in a spirit of faith. The point of the gospel is that for the first generation of Christians it was just as it is for us: the gospel and even the resurrection of Jesus, the heart of the gospel, must be taken on faith. The number of persons who actually saw the risen Lord was not very large—and in comparison to the total number of Christians, then and now, was infinitesimal: "Blessed are those who have not seen and yet believe." This blessedness, this beatitude, is ours.

Finally, it is part of our Easter consolation to perceive what Christ's risen life is like. It is first of all a life of concern for others: for the twelve, his friends, and through them for the whole world. This is the life we are to share. The peace of forgiveness which, through his disciples, has spread from him to us is to go from us to all.

Third Sunday of Easter

Reading 1: Acts 5:27b–32, 40b–41
Responsorial: Psalm 30:1, 3, 4–5, 10–11a, 12b
Reading 2: Revelation 5:11–14
Gospel: John 21:1–19

is seated at the right hand of the Father
one holy . . . apostolic Church
his kingdom will have no end

    The gospel reports another appearance of the risen Jesus to his disciples. He comes to them, is identified, and eats with them a meal he himself prepares, of charcoal-broiled fish and bread.
    But, as last week, the thoughts of the risen Jesus are not only on the twelve disciples, but on those to whom these first disciples must be sent. So he asks of Peter a threefold confession of love. The request is first of all for Peter's sake, so he can know he is forgiven his threefold denial. But it is also for all those to whom Peter and the other apostles will be sent: the sheep entrusted to their care. Jesus says, "Feed my sheep," entrusting the church to Peter's attention and care. The risen life of the Christian is to be a life within this community, of which Peter is shepherd because he loves Christ. If he loves Christ he is to feed Christ's lambs and sheep. To the extent that he loves Christ, his love is to show itself and spread itself over

those who belong to Christ. Ruling in the name of Christ means loving, and the measure of the rule is the greatness of the love. The supreme pastor is proud to assume the title, "Servant of the servants of God."

The gospel also indicates in its closing words the death by which Peter was to glorify God. That is, his hands would be stretched out and bound, as had been the hands of Jesus in his trial; and Peter too would be dragged to a martyr's death. Our "one holy catholic Church" is, we say, "apostolic." That is, it is built on the foundations of the apostles and the martyrs. Peter was both an apostle and a martyr.

The gospel reports that, "Jesus revealed himself"—as one who loves and who seeks love. With him is "the disciple whom Jesus loved"—who is never given a name in the gospel, because he stands for all of us. And there is Peter, of whom Jesus asks three times, "Do you love me?" Only when Peter pledges his love does Jesus commission him to care for his church: "Feed my lambs. . . . Feed my sheep."

Jesus reveals himself as one who cares for his own. He provides food for them, cooks it with his own hands. He serves it to them: "He came and took the bread and gave it to them, and so with the fish."

Then Jesus reveals his concern for all those to whom these disciples will take his word. He asks Peter for a testimony of preeminence in love: "Do you love me more than these others do?" If Peter loves Jesus more, then Peter automatically has more responsibility for loving and serving the least of Jesus' brethren: "As long as you did it to the least of these my brothers and sisters, you did it to me." "Do you love me? Feed my lambs. . . . Feed my sheep."

The risen life is not just floating around in clouds of glory. The risen life, seeking "the things that are above where Christ is seated at the right hand of God" (Colossians 3:1), remains a life of loving concern for all. Christ did not consider his life above, in "equality with God, a thing to be grasped, but emptied himself, taking the form of a servant" (Philippians 2:6f). "Though he was rich, yet for your sake he became poor" (2 Corinthians 8:9). So now Christ, even though risen from the dead and ascended to the right hand of the Father, is con-

Third Sunday : 93

cerned for our good: "Behold I am with you always, to the close of the age" (Matthew 28:20); "I will not leave you desolate; I will come to you" (John 14:18). In the same way, Christ's saints in the risen life are concerned for us. Their prayers can and do help us below. This is part of what we call "the communion of saints."

Notice that Jesus reveals himself especially in serving them the bread: as in Luke's story about what happened the evening of the first Easter. The risen Jesus walked along the road with two disciples who did not recognize him. He finally revealed himself to them "in the breaking of the bread" (Luke 24:35, gospel for an evening mass on Easter day). The early Christians, the first generation in particular, felt Jesus' presence particularly keenly at the eucharistic meals they held together; we, too, find him present in our Eucharist.

The theme of the life of the apostle and martyr appears also in today's passage from Acts. Being an apostle and martyr is a part of sharing Christ's risen life. In the first days of the church, Peter and the other apostles began at once fulfilling Jesus' commission to them, preaching to all the good news of Christ. The leaders of the people forbade them to preach any more, but they said they must obey God rather than men. They repeated their message before the Council itself: "the God of our fathers raised Jesus, whom you killed by hanging him on a tree. God exalted him at his right hand as Leader and Savior, to give repentance to Israel and forgiveness of sins." The Council did not simply charge them; it held them in prison; it had them beaten and charged them again. Then the apostles "rejoiced they were counted worthy to suffer dishonor for the name. And every day in the temple and at home they did not cease preaching in the name of Jesus."

Thus was founded and born the church apostolic mentioned in the Creed. It begins with the preaching, under the threat of martyrdom for the name of Jesus, by the first apostles in the power of the resurrection, which they had experienced, and which they now tried to share with all in faith and wonder.

The selection from Revelation is a glimpse of heavenly glory. In the center of it all is "the Lamb who was slain." The lamb is "the lamb of God, who takes away the sins of the world"; that is, it is Jesus, the true paschal lamb, symbolized and foretold in the Old Testament ritual. At this first new Passover, instead of a lamb being slain in sacrifice and its blood being used to mark those who were saved, Jesus offers himself in sacrifice, and his blood becomes the sign of God's salvation for all who believe.

In the Creed we say, "On the third day he rose again in fulfillment of the Scriptures; he ascended into heaven and is seated at the right hand of the Father." This passage from Revelation is an attempt to portray what that might mean. The author sees Jesus as the lamb, now in glory, but still bearing the marks of his suffering. To him all those in heaven sing a new song, saying, "Worthy art thou, for thou wast slain and by thy blood didst ransom men for God from every tribe and tongue and people and nation, and hast made them a kingdom and priests to our God, and they shall reign on earth."

Easter Preface 3 uses this lamb theme: "Christ is the victim who dies now no more; the Lamb, once slain, who lives forever." So does Easter Preface 5: "As he gave himself into your hands for our salvation, he showed himself to be the priest, the altar, and the lamb of sacrifice. . . . "As he offered his body on the cross, his perfect sacrifice fulfilled all others." And so, "we praise you with greater joy than ever in this Easter season, when Christ became our paschal sacrifice."

All of these Easter Scriptures are efforts to convey the spirit of this great central feast of the church year. Here more than anywhere else is the heart of our religion. The center and substance of our whole faith is in those central lines of the Creed concerning Christ's suffering and exaltation.

These readings are intended to bring that confession of faith to life for us, to give us something of the profound meaning in those few lines, so easily memorized, so quickly repeated in prayer. But conveying that meaning is not easy. It concerns not only the distant past and remote future, but is especially concerned with the present. Death and resurrection are daily realities; we experience them.

For instance, the psalm of today's mass praises the Lord for having rescued the speaker. The rescue is described as a resurrection: "Thou hast drawn me up, thou hast brought up my soul from Sheol, restored me to life from among those gone down to the Pit." Neither David nor any other songwriter of Israel had literally died and been restored to life, returning from the pit of Sheol. But God's rescue in many instances of daily life—rescue from disease, from the dangers of battle, from extreme losses of poverty or failure—could be experienced and recounted as so many returns from the dead.

There is a similar use of language in much of our Christian literature, because the basic idea of cross and resurrection provides a theme which runs through life and a way of looking in faith at every problem that can arise. No matter what the suffering, challenge, or risk, we accept it as from God's hand. We face it or endure it, as the circumstances demand, and look forward in faith to the transformation God is working in us through it.

This recurring pattern of salvation is the pattern of Christ applied to our lives. At Easter time especially we rejoice that it has been so clearly revealed.

Fourth Sunday of Easter

Reading 1: Acts 13:14, 43–52

Responsorial: Psalm 100:1–2, 3, 5

Reading 2: Revelation 7:9, 14b–17

Gospel: John 10:27–30

We believe in one holy catholic and apostolic Church.

*We look for the resurrection of the dead,
and the life of the world to come.*

the communion of saints

We continue the readings from the Acts of the Apostles and from the book of Revelation. Acts today takes us to some of the first preaching of Paul and Barnabas. Through their trials, God was building his church. In each of the towns here named, they went into the local synagogue and began to preach that Jesus was the Christ. If they ran into trouble, contradictions, and even persecution, Paul said, "All right; if you will not let us speak peaceably in the synagogue, we will go outside and preach where not only Jews but also gentiles can hear us." Through those first rejections, the church began to spread. When active persecution followed and they were driven from one district, they fled to another and preached there. Meanwhile, converts they had made bore testimony under persecution and so still others were attracted to the faith.

Here we see again the apostolic beginnings of the "one holy catholic . . . Church." In those beginnings, as so often in Scripture, we also see the pattern of successful operations of the church through the centuries. That is, the church typically does what it can, plans and preaches and exerts itself to do God's work in whatever way seems best. But God always has his own designs. Even more important than what we, as the church, accomplish for God by our own efforts, is our readiness to see his hand in all that befalls us, even when our efforts are being contradicted, frustrated, reviled. (It is no more than Jesus foretold.) Then if, under necessity, we flee from persecution—or suffer and bear it or are killed in it—then, today as in the first days, God uses the blood of martyrs as the seed of Christians. He gives the increase. Thus the church is more his than ours. By suffering and persecution, "through many tribulations we must enter the kingdom of God" (Acts 14:22). This too is implied in our sharing Christ's risen life. The gospel is not just resurrection, but death and resurrection.

The reading from the book of Revelation tells of the saints who stand before God. It is, we observe gratefully, "a great multitude which no man could number, from every nation, from all tribes and peoples and tongues." We hope to be in their number, when all those saints come marching in.

They are, in this vision, clothed in white robes, having "washed them white in the blood of the Lamb." Of course in the world as we know it washing something in blood does not make it white. But in spite of that the symbolism is not obscure. The idea is that Jesus' self-sacrifice makes holy and pure all those who join themselves to it by their faith and baptism: "We acknowledge one baptism for the forgiveness of sins." They carry palm branches in their hands: the well-known symbol of victory. "These are they who have come out of the great tribulation" and have emerged victors. Instead of being conquered by "the beast" and all the oppressions and temptations of this world, they have themselves overcome, even, if necessary, by shedding their own blood. As is explained in chapter three of the book of Revelation, "He who conquers shall be clad in white garments . . . they shall walk with me in white, for they are worthy." In chapters two and three many promises were made to those who conquer: they will eat of the tree of life, which is in the paradise of God; they will not be hurt by the second death; they will be given some of the hidden manna, and a white stone with a new name written on the stone; they will be given power over the nations to rule them with a rod of iron; they will be given the morning star; their names will not be blotted from the book of life; Jesus will confess their name before his Father and before his angels. He will make them to be pillars in the temple of God, with his own name and God's name and the name of the new Jerusalem written thereon.

Here the vision shows still further rewards heaped upon the saints who have triumphed: they are before the throne of God; they serve him night and day within his temple; and he who sits upon the throne (God) will shelter them with his presence.

> They shall hunger no more, neither thirst any more; the sun shall not strike them, nor any scorching heat. For the Lamb in the midst of the throne will be their shepherd, and he will guide them to springs of living water; and God will wipe away every tear from their eyes.

All these are further promises for us, who hope to be in their number.

Finally, in the gospel, we have a selection from Jesus' instruction on the good shepherd. The good shepherd lays down his life for his sheep, and that is what Jesus has done. Jesus, who has been introduced as "the lamb of God" by John the Baptist, here speaks about his sheep, of which he is the shepherd. Both images, Jesus as shepherd and as lamb, were combined in the passage we just read: "the Lamb in the midst of the throne will be their shepherd."

At any rate, the message of the gospel is clear: "I give them eternal life, and they shall never perish; and no one shall snatch them out of my hand." Christ's power is the power of God—"I and the Father are one." Therefore none can stand against him. Those who are his are safe.

But who are his? Only those who are willing to go through what he did. Only those who resist being conquered by world and flesh and devil. They are the ones, members of the communion of saints, who will have eternal life safe in his hands: "He will come again in glory to judge the living and the dead, and his kingdom will have no end. We look for the resurrection of the dead and the life of the world to come."

Fifth Sunday of Easter

Reading 1: Acts 14:21–27

Responsorial: Psalm 145:8–9, 10–11, 12–13ab

Reading 2: Revelation 21:1–5a

Gospel: John 13:31–33a, 34–35

We believe in one holy . . . and apostolic Church.

the communion of saints

*We look for the resurrection of the dead,
and the life of the world to come.*

    Today's reading from the Acts of the Apostles tells how the message in the very earliest preaching was "through many tribulations we must enter the kingdom of God." These were preachers who had themselves experienced Christ risen. They knew what the fullness of the gift of the Holy Spirit meant, for they had received it. They wrote of themselves that they were dead with Christ and risen with him; that they had with him ascended on high into heavenly places. But they still knew that, true as all this was, it did not cancel the need of their living with Christ and dying with Christ so they might fully rise and reign with him.

    So the preachers of the resurrection are at the same time preachers of the cross: "through many tribulations we must enter the kingdom of God." But the cross they preach has already been touched with glory. Cross, suffering, and death no longer cause fear. They can even be thought of with joy, because our Lord has undergone them. He, through whom all things were made, suffered, died, and was buried, and on the third day rose again. Now his kingdom will have no end, and we will share in that kingdom—to the extent that we have been privileged to share in that sacrifice, tribulation, humiliation unto death.

With this preaching, "they appointed elders for them in every church," organizing Christ's church from city to city, town to town, laying on hands, beginning what would become our apostolic succession. Bishops and elders of today (elders or presbyters—the ones we commonly call priests) continue in the mission, the work and the life-commission of the first apostles, evangelists, and martyrs.

The selection from Revelation is the vision of the final happiness, described insofar as words can describe something like that. John says he saw a new heaven and a new earth, after the passing of the first heaven and the first earth and the sea. He saw the holy city, the new Jerusalem, coming out of heaven from God, prepared as a bride adorned for her husband. The life to come is described as life in the new Jerusalem; that is, in the dwelling of God with his people: "He will dwell with them and they shall be his people, and God himself will be with them."

Now we notice at once that this is very like what has already been said in the gospel of John, where it is said to have already happened: "And the Word became flesh, and dwelt among us; and we saw his glory, glory as of the only-begotten of the Father." So, in some ways, we possess heaven already. Or, perhaps better expressed, the heaven we shall possess will not be essentially different from, will be the natural development of, the heaven we already have here if we indeed know Christ.

At any rate, the words of complete consolation are very beautiful and worth remembering: "He will wipe away every tear from their eyes, and death shall be no more. For the former things have passed away. . . . Behold, I make all things new." That is the great promise. For this, "we look for the resurrection of the dead and the life of the world to come." We refer to this when we say, "he will come again in glory . . and his kingdom will have no end."

Finally, the key to the new and risen life was given by Jesus to his disciples the night before he died. He talked to them then for a long time about how, even after his death, he would always be with them; and about how he would live in them in his Spirit. But the means of their sharing all this was what he called his new commandment. It is in the living of his new commandment that we most come to life in him and that we truly overcome death. It is because of his new commandment that we are willing to do as he did, face any risk, even that of death. The new commandment is simple, powerful, direct, unmistakable: "that you love one another even as I have loved you, that you also love one another." Besides the commandment, he gives them the sign by which they will be known. Not a password, not a secret handshake, not a mystical ceremony, but simply, "By this all men will know that you are my disciples, if you have love for one another." Not only is that statement too clear to require comment, it is also an embarrassingly specific measure of the quality of our discipleship.

These are the words Jesus speaks as he goes to his death. And it is the content of these words that makes his death what he calls it: being glorified. To go to death in love and obedience is to find true glory. That is what he did, and it is this glory that he calls us to share. By that glory he will judge us too when he comes "again in glory to judge the living and the dead." That is the measure of our lives: his life.

It is important to see that his glory is not something tacked on to the miseries of this life. It is the transformation of those miseries. Christ is glorified in suffering, on the cross. That is what he promises us.

Sixth Sunday of Easter

Reading 1: Acts 15:1–2, 22–29

Responsorial: Psalm 67:1–2, 4, 5, 7

Reading 2: Revelation 21:10–14, 22–23

Gospel: John 14:23–29

one holy catholic and apostolic Church

    The reading from Acts shows another step in the development of the first Christian community. Like many other developments since, it had its origin in a disagreement and a quarrel within the community. (It might be a consolation to us to reflect on the fact that the risen life of love, even in the first Christian generation, was not so perfect as to rule out all dissension. We read today that "Paul and Barnabas had no small dissension and debate with them." And only a few verses later, in a section not quoted in our Sunday readings, we learn that between Paul and Barnabas themselves "there arose a sharp contention, so that they separated from one another" [Acts 15:30]).

    The good result of this particular argument was that it forced them to find a way to settle important arguments definitively. What they invented was essentially the idea of a church council and of an appeal to "headquarters." Headquarters then was in Jerusalem, and so in Jerusalem Peter and the twelve and the elders (or presbyters) of the community, and the whole body of the faithful (insofar as this was possible) came together to discuss the problem and to come to a decision on it. When they did come to the decision, they announced it to the rest of the church as not only theirs, but as the decision of "the Holy Spirit": "It has seemed good to the Holy Spirit and to us." Big words, are they not? But we have learned that our belief in the Holy Spirit includes belief in his having spoken through the prophets, and also includes belief in "one holy catholic and apostolic Church." The Holy Spirit expresses himself in action when the church comes together in a formal, explicit way and reaches a definitive decision on what is to be done or to be believed.

It is also interesting to us that the decision reached at that council—a very important decision, on which the whole life of the church seemed to hang—also was in the long run to be only a temporary decision. That is, they made a compromise with observance of the Jewish law, a compromise we no longer observe.

The compromise was in agreeing with one party that circumcision and the overall observance of the law would not be required of Christians who were not themselves Jews while also agreeing that some of the more significant and visible legal observances should be maintained. Christians would not eat food which had been sacrificed to idols, for instance. That meant, in general, that they could not safely buy just any food in the open market, because much of that food came from pagan temples, was often ritually consecrated to some god, and later sold in the public markets for the support of the temple.

Secondly, Christians could not eat blood. British "black pudding" and German blood sausage would obviously not have developed in a Christendom living under Acts 15. But more than that, the law might have required Christians to be as careful as observant Jews about buying only kosher meat to be sure that what they ate had been drained of blood. At any rate, Christians under Acts 15 had to abstain totally from a third kind of food, things strangled, for they had to contain blood. But strangling was the ordinary way to kill many fowl which were quite popular foods.

Finally, the compromise demanded that they keep themselves from unchastity. This, of course, could not mean simply sins against the sixth commandment, or the decree would seem to imply that sins against any other commandment were acceptable—which is absurd. The decree certainly means some special kind of unchastity which could be incurred according to the Jewish law but not otherwise. For instance, it could refer to the specific regulations governing marriage within certain degrees of kinship, laws requiring certain observances in the timing of marital relations, or laws forbidding marriage of Jews with gentiles.

We no longer observe these proscriptions, but those early Christians did. For instance, we have evidence from Christian writings at least as late as the third century that Christians still felt obliged to avoid eating blood. That, then, was a Christian belief for a period at least as long as the entire history of the United States. Yet the rule was eventually dropped completely. Changes in the church did not begin with the Second Vatican Council.

The reading from Revelation is a further description of the heavenly glory. The holy city of Jerusalem is pictured as a great jewel, a shining crystal. It has three gates on each of four sides—gates open therefore to all four directions of the compass, to all the nations of the earth. As we saw earlier, those saved are a great crowd which none could number, from all tribes and nations and tongues. And the city of the saved is founded on twelve foundations, which have the names of the twelve apostles of the Lamb. The passage suggests not only the apostolic origin of the church, but also its catholic aspect of openness to all peoples, as did the first reading about moving from the exclusively Jewish law.

The first reading also stressed unity through the appeal to the apostolic council, and here the unity of the one church is emphasized by mention of its one common foundation and its one encircling wall.

Finally there is the beautiful description of the city itself, a city in which God himself is the temple, the Lamb is its lamp, and the light he sheds is the glory of God. Therefore there is no need of sun or moon to shine upon it.

The gospel continues with a selection from Jesus' last words to his disciples. The words breathe the special spirit of the risen life he is promising to believers. It will be a life in love. But if we love and keep Jesus' command to love one another as he has loved us, then a marvelous effect will take place: the Father will love us and Father and Son will come to us and will make their home with us. But he warns as well: not to keep his word, not to observe his commandment to love all others as he has loved us, is to show that we do not truly love him.

The risen life will be also a life in the Holy Spirit, whom "the Father will send in my name." It will be a life in which "the Counselor, the Spirit . . . will teach you all things." It will be a life in peace; not in trouble, in spite of Jesus' death and absence. It will be a life of joy, because of our knowledge that he is with the Father.

Ascension

Reading 1: Acts 1:1–11

Responsorial: Psalm 47:1–2, 5–6, 7–8

Reading 2: Ephesians 1:17–23

Gospel: Luke 24:46–53

*he ascended into heaven
and is seated at the right hand of the Father*

    The ascension is a major article of the Creed: "He ascended into heaven." But that article does not stand alone. For its meaning, we must take it together with the following two statements: "and is seated at the right hand of the Father. He will come again in glory."
    That is the way we see the ascension presented in today's story from Acts: "while they were looking on, he was lifted up, and a cloud took him out of their sight." Then two angels—the two men in white robes who suddenly appear—say, "Why do you stand looking up to heaven? This Jesus, who was taken up from you into heaven will come in the same way as you saw him go into heaven."
    Jesus had foretold, "Then they will see the Son of Man coming in a cloud with power and great glory. Now when these things begin to take place, look up and raise your heads, because your redemption is drawing near" (Luke 21:27f). Jesus also spoke of the day when "the Son of Man comes in his glory and the glory of the Father and of the holy angels" (Luke

9:26). "As the lightning flashes and lights up the sky from one side to the other, so will the Son of Man be in his day" (Luke 17:24), "the day when the Son of Man will be revealed" (Luke 17:30). But before that day, "he must suffer many things and be rejected by this generation" (Luke 17:25).

We celebrate a day when Jesus' suffering and rejection are past. He is raised to glory. In the course of his passion (Luke 22:67–71), the Council had asked him, "If you are the Christ, tell us." But he said to them, "If I tell you, you will not believe, and if I ask you you will not answer. But from now on the Son of Man shall be seated at the right hand of the power of God." His questioners knew what that meant. "They all said, 'Are you the Son of God, then?'" They knew that saying he would be seated at the right hand of God was a claim that he was the Son of God, a claim they considered blasphemy, worthy of death.

But this is our belief: that he who once came to us and walked among us as one of us, is, after having been killed by us, now in glory as God's Son. We believe he will come again, this time not in human lowliness, but in glory as God's Son. We wait for that day, as for the time when all fair judgment will take place—that is, we wait for it if we have given our lives to him and tried to live by his judgment.

The letter to the Ephesians sums this up. It is a prayer for God to enlighten our hearts that we may know the hope to which we are called. How shall we know it? By appreciating "the working of his great might which he accomplished in Christ." What he accomplished in Christ is "the measure of the riches of his glorious inheritance in the saints." That is the measure of "the immeasurable greatness of his power in us who believe."

And what did God accomplish in Christ? He "raised him from the dead and made him sit at his right hand in the heavenly places." That means he gave Christ a position "far above all rule and authority and power and dominion." That means Christ's name is placed "above every name that is named, not only in this age but also in the age to come." It means God has placed all things under Christ's feet.

This is what God did with the one who was, at the age of

thirty-three, arrested, imprisoned, legally condemned and sentenced, tortured to death in a public execution, buried, and forgotten. This is what God promises to do for us, this he says we may hope for from him, these are riches we can inherit, this is the power which can be at work in us. For we are a part of Christ; that is, he is now "the head over all things for the church, which is his body." We are the church, his body. We are "the fullness of him who fills all in all."

And when will we receive all these wonderful things? As part of his body, we have them already as our right and inheritance and belonging. In experienced, full reality, we shall have them most perfectly when he does come again in glory to judge all things justly and fairly.

The gospel explains to the apostles for the first time in its fullness the message they will preach to all nations. Jesus shows them how it truly fulfills the Scriptures they had been reading all their lives: "It is written that the Christ should suffer and on the third day rise from the dead, and that repentance and forgiveness of sins should be preached in his name to all nations, beginning from Jerusalem." He tells them to be witnesses of these things to all the world, but first to remain in Jerusalem "until you are clothed with power from on high"; that is, until the Spirit comes upon them, which will happen at Pentecost.

A modern reader, of course, wants to know if all these things are to be believed as literally happening. Did the apostles stand there on a given day and watch Jesus rise up from the earth, like a balloon, like a rocket, like Superman?

The best way to judge is to start with the statement, "is seated at the right hand of the Father." We know there is no such thing as the right hand of God. God is a spirit, and has no right or left, top or bottom, front or back. People knew that perfectly well when the gospel was written. Their notion of God was probably more spiritual than our own.

Why, then, did they say Jesus is seated at the right hand of God if they knew God had no right hand? Because that was a perfectly good expression for what Jesus claims at the close of the gospel of Matthew: "All power is given me in heaven and on earth." They wanted to say he is exalted. Very exalted. He is in the highest imaginable position. He is in the very reverse of the miserable state in which our eyes saw him suffer and die and be buried. He is not just dead like a dog, thrown aside and forgotten. He has a share in the very divinity of God, the power and glory of God the Father. So they said he is enthroned with God the Father, ruling over all; or, in other words, in the language used for earthly kings, he is seated at God's right hand. God does not have a right hand; God has no throne. But God rules over all, so we say he is enthroned. And as God is enthroned, so Christ is enthroned.

If we can be sure of what they meant when they said Christ was "seated at the right hand of the Father," we can also understand what they meant when they said "he ascended into heaven." Ascending into heaven was moving to his place at God's right hand. It means that his earthly career was now over: he had left this sphere of existence. He was now in the state of fulfilled glory to which we ourselves look forward.

This is what we find in the opening prayer of the mass today:

> Father in heaven, when you took Christ beyond our sight, our minds were prepared for the coming of your kingdom. May we follow where he has led, and find our hope in his glory. May we follow him into the new creation, for his ascension is our glory and our hope.

The prayer over the gifts and the prayer after communion both refer to following him with love to eternal life, rising with him to the joys of heaven. Finally the solemn blessing proclaims his ascension to prepare a place for us. But these prayers remind us too of when he will appear as judge, and that, though he has ascended to the Father, he is also with us and can be experienced as with us, to the end of time.

Seventh Sunday of Easter

Reading 1: Acts 7:55–60

Responsorial: Psalm 97:1, 2b, 6, 7c, 9

Reading 2: Revelation: 22:12–14, 16–17, 20

Gospel: John 17:20–26

He will come again in glory to judge the living and the dead

Church

The reading from Acts is again a witness to the life of the early church: the readiness for martyrdom in boldly proclaiming their faith; the spirit of love after the model of Jesus himself, which they tried to practice. Stephen forgives those who are putting him to death, exactly as Jesus had prayed for the forgiveness of his executioners (Luke 23:24). And in his doing so, his blood became the seed of more Christians, for the young man named Saul is soon to be converted to the apostle Paul.

At his trial, Stephen experiences what Jesus had foretold: a vision of Christ in glory. Stephen says, "I see the heavens opened and the Son of Man standing at the right hand of God." But they are his last words, and he is himself hurried to his death.

Like many others Christians before and since, Stephen may have pondered the prophecies of Christ's second coming and wondered if he himself would live to see it. Now at the moment of his death he could realize that this was Christ's coming for him; *now* was the moment his world was about to end.

The same thing is true of us. The coming of Christ which we can certainly expect is his coming to each of us at the moment of death—which may not be very far off for any one of us. Then we shall see him in glory, ready to judge us according to our readiness now to judge ourselves and our world by his standards.

The reading from Revelation is a vivid promise of Christ's early return "to repay everyone for what he has done." Christ will come bringing my recompense. And the proper Christian response is that of the Spirit and the bride (the Spirit and the church). They say, "Come." And Jesus' last words, closing the book and the entire Bible are, "Surely I am coming soon." Our response is given: it is, "Amen. Come, Lord Jesus."

And what of the meantime? The prayers of today's mass concentrate on this time. It is not a time of vision. But neither is it a time of distant separation and of loneliness. With his ascension, Christ has begun another kind of existence, but he has not abandoned us. On the contrary, as the prayer for today's mass says, "Help us keep in mind that Christ our Savior lives with you in glory and promised to remain with us until the end of time." It is a prayer "that we may recognize the presence of Christ in our midst."

The gospel text leads our thoughts in the same direction with Jesus' prayer of concern for us in the inbetween time. It is a prayer, he says, "not for these only"—that is, the disciples in the same room with him the night before he died—"but also for those who believe in me through their word—that is, for us, the millions of other Christians through the ages. What is his prayer for us? It is "that they may all be one." He wants us to be one, not like the members of any club, not even like the members of a single family, but still more perfectly one. All Christians, his body on earth, "the communion of saints," the "one holy catholic and apostolic Church," he wants to be one, "even as thou, Father, art in me and I in thee, that they also may be one in us, that the world may believe that thou hast sent me." He expands and repeats that prayer: "that they may be one, even as we are one, I in them and thou in me, that they may become perfectly one, so that the world may know that thou hast sent me. . . ."

As a prayer for our perfect unity, this is also a prayer for our perfect love among ourselves: "By this will all men know that you are my disciples, that you have love for one another" (John 13:35). By this will he judge us when he comes again to judge the living and the dead. To this end is he now directing the world from his throne above, to make us one. If we do this, we make clear that God's love is in us as it was in Jesus. God has offered his love to us in sending us his only Son to die on the cross for our salvation, that we "who believe in him may not perish but may have eternal life" (John 3:16).

So Jesus prays also for the inbetween time that "they also whom thou hast given me may be with me where I am to behold my glory which thou hast given me. . . ." He is saying this the night before he died—and the glory of which he speaks is first the glory of the cross. There we are to be with him and there we are to come to know his glory, the glory "which thou hast given me in love before the foundation of the world." But if we join him there, then "the love with which thou hast loved me" will be in us, and he will be in us.

Pentecost Sunday

Reading 1: Acts 2:1–11

Responsorial: Psalm 104:1ab, 24ac, 29bc–30, 31, 34

Reading 2: 1 Corinthians 12:3b–7, 12–13

Gospel: John 20:19–23

With the Father and the Son he is worshiped and glorified.

Today is the feast of the coming of the Spirit. In the reading from Acts we see how it first happened: tongues of fire came down on all present and they began to speak in other tongues as the Spirit gave utterance. In the power of the Spirit, the preaching began, the telling of the Christian story and the praising of these mighty works of God.

In 1 Corinthians 12, the workings of the Spirit are seen again. All we do that is good, all that contributes to the building of the church, the body of Christ, in love and service, is a work of God manifesting his Spirit, the Spirit of God, the Spirit of Jesus. In the Spirit we are baptized into one body with other persons from all conceivable backgrounds. But among all the different members of the body, there is one Spirit of love and peace.

This is the Spirit of whom we say in the Creed, "with the Father and the Son, he is worshiped and glorified." The works of the Spirit are the works of God. The presence of the Spirit which we feel is the presence of God. The one God is three divine persons: Father, Son, and Spirit. These three are one and equal and are in one another and share in one another's works. The Spirit of love proceeds from Father and Son together: one love comes from both; they are not two sources of love but one source. When we receive the Spirit, that divine love begins to live in us. Where the Spirit is present and active, there the church of Christ begins to rise. So we celebrate Pentecost as the birthday of the church.

To learn about the Holy Spirit, there is perhaps no better way than to meditate slowly the Sequence of today's mass. The Spirit is light divine, giver of all God's gifts, consoler, comforter, healer. He is source of all in us that is good; he is fountain of grace. His seven gifts are the height of the Christian life: wisdom, knowledge, understanding, counsel, piety, fortitude, fear of the Lord.

Trinity Sunday: Sunday after Pentecost

Reading 1: Proverbs 8:22–31

Responsorial: Psalm 8:3–4, 5–6a, 6b–8

Reading 2: Romans 5:1–5

Gospel: John 16:12–15

We believe in . . . God, the Father
   in one Lord, Jesus Christ
   in the Holy Spirit

This is the day when it is best simply to be silent and worship without words; for this is the day honoring the most profound mystery of our faith, the blessed Trinity. There is one God, and only one God: "Hear, O Israel, the Lord our God is one Lord . . . (Deuteronomy 6:4). Even to suspect otherwise is to violate the first of the commandments: "You shall have no other gods before me" (Deuteronomy 5:7).

Moreover, the one true God is the most profound unity: not like ourselves, and the things we know, made up of parts. God simply *is;* he never had to be put together. He is just there, the fullness of reality, fact, truth: "I AM who I AM." That is the only name he wants.

But we say we believe in Jesus Christ, God's only Son, our Lord, "eternally begotten of the Father." Born of what Father? Of God, the only true God. There is only one God. Yet we believe that Jesus is "God from God, Light from Light, true God from true God." But there are not two gods, but only one true God. For God's Son is "begotten not made; one in Being with the Father." Yet the Son is not the Father. The Son became man and died on the cross. The Father did not become man and did not die on the cross. The Son is God. The Father is God. But there is only one God.

And we also believe "in the Holy Spirit, the Lord, the Giver of life, who proceeds from the Father and the Son." The Son is begotten of the Father; the Spirit proceeds from the Father and the Son. "With the Father and the Son, he is worshiped and glorified." That is, the Holy Spirit, who proceeds from God, is God. As God he is "glorified and worshiped," just as are the Father and the Son. But there is only one God.

So, each of the three persons is God. The Spirit is not the Father. The Spirit is not the Son. But the Spirit is God. When Jesus prayed, he said, "Father." For instance, "Father, into thy hands I commend my spirit" (Luke 23:46); "I thank thee, Father, Lord of heaven and earth" (Luke 10:21). He taught us, when we pray, to address "our Father in heaven," and we do that faithfully. When we speak to God our Father, the Father of our Lord Jesus Christ, we speak as brothers and sisters of Jesus, living by the love of his Holy Spirit. So in the prayer of today's mass we say, "Father, you sent your Word to bring us truth and your Spirit to make us holy."

The Son and the Spirit have missions; that is, they are sent, in ways characteristic of who they are. The Spirit is sent by the Father and the Son, because the Spirit proceeds from both of them. The Son, or Word, is sent by the Father, because he is begotten by the Father. The Father is never sent.

The Father has no mission because in the Trinity he is the origin of the other two persons. In this sense, and in this sense only, are we to take Christ's words, "The Father is greater than I" (John 14:28). In all other senses, all three persons are completely equal: as Jesus said in another place, "The Father and I are one" (John 10:30). They are one in power, one in divinity, one in knowledge, one in eternity. They are equal but distinct as persons. This is a mystery of our faith. We worship in silence.

The first reading is a selection from Proverbs, spoken in the person of the wisdom of God. What is the wisdom of God?

How can the wisdom of God speak and tell us about itself, and say "I existed before the beginning of the earth; I was with God when he made the world; I was beside him like a master workman"?

God is wise, and he always was wise and always will be wise. So God's wisdom is as eternal as God himself. So is God's love and God's beauty. In fact, we say God's love is God, and God is love. God's beauty is God, and God is beauty. God's wisdom is God, and God is wisdom. Describing God and his attributes, his virtues, his various qualities, therefore, sounds somewhat like describing God and the three persons of the blessed Trinity.

Therefore, when Christians found this text in the Old Testament book of Proverbs describing God's wisdom, they thought it was very close to a good account of what they meant by God's Son, the Word of God; so, reading it today, we realize that long before the time of Christ there were certain things said and written in the Old Testament which to us can suggest the great truth of the Trinity. This passage, fittingly for the Word which became flesh and dwelt among us, says, "I was daily his delight, rejoicing before him always, rejoicing in his inhabited world, and delighting in the sons of men." The passage also says that God's wisdom was before God and with God, "like a master workman." That means, of course, that when God created, he created by his own wisdom and according to the pattern of his own wisdom. But it fits what we believe of our one Lord, Jesus Christ, the only Son of God, that "through him all things were made."

Today's reading from Romans describes our relations with the triune God: "God's love has been poured forth into our hearts through the Holy Spirit who has been given to us." Why do we have God's love, and why indeed has the Holy Spirit been given to us? Because "we have peace with God through our Lord Jesus Christ." We have this peace through Christ by our faith. This we have seen in earlier meditations on Romans. By our faith that Christ suffered and died and rose from the dead for our salvation, we are justified, and we share in Christ's life of love and sonship.

In the gospel lesson Jesus tells his disciples of the Spirit of truth who will come to them and guide them into all truth: the Spirit "will take what is mine and declare it to you."

What Jesus has and calls his own is all that the Father has and calls his own: "All that the Father has is mine; therefore I said that he [the Spirit] will take what is mine and declare it to you." In other words, the one true God has made himself known in Jesus, his Son, in his life on earth, especially in his suffering, death, and resurrection; and now, in the ages after Jesus' own life on earth, the Spirit of God, the Holy Spirit of truth, who proceeds from the Father and the Son, remains with us, in our hearts, in our community of faith, the church, and guides us into all truth about God revealed in the life of Jesus.

This is the great mystery of the Trinity, one God in three divine persons. Three divine persons in one God. "Glory to the Father, the Son and the Holy Spirit, to God who is, who was, and who is to come. Alleluja" (the gospel invocation).

Ninth Sunday of the Year

Reading 1: 1 Kings 8:41–43

Responsorial: Psalm 117:1, 2

Reading 2: Galatians 1:1–2, 6–10

Gospel: Luke 7:1–10

one . . . catholic . . . Church

The issue in today's readings is the universality of salvation. It is the issue we touch when, in the Creed, we say we believe the church is catholic. 'Catholic' means "universal, for all." The reading from 1 Kings cites Solomon's prayer in dedicating the temple he had just built, and includes Solomon's wish that God's temple in Jerusalem will be a house of prayer for all peoples. If the church, as Christ's body, has become God's living temple in this new age, it too must be open to all peoples and provide easy access to God for all.

The response for the psalm emphasizes the universality of the message: "Go out to all the world, and tell the Good News"; while the psalm itself calls on all nations, all peoples, to praise and extol the Lord.

But a grave threat to universality arose in the early church. That threat is behind Paul's writing to the Galatians about "a different gospel," "another gospel," "a gospel contrary to that which we preached to you." Paul had preached the universality of salvation. Contrary to much of Old Testament law, he held that one need not become a Jew and observe all the ritual and cleanliness practices of the Jewish religion in order to be saved. The law was good and holy, but it had been given, according to Paul, to keep Israel on the right path of a good life until the fullness of God's message should come in Christ (Galatians 3:23–29). Gentiles who entered the church should be instructed in salvation through the full acceptance of Christ's cross and resurrection. But they need not accept the observance of the Old Testament law.

Not all Paul's fellow Christians agreed. Most of the first generation of Christians were Jewish, and many of them had been believers longer than Paul had. Some of them came to Galatia and pointed out to Paul's converts those passages of the Bible which clearly insisted on total observance of the law. The young Galatian churches wanted to be real Christians, so they began to worry whether or not Paul had withheld from them half the truth about Christianity.

Paul's point of view eventually prevailed in the church; Christianity since then has not been dependent on one's accepting Judaism and all the observances of Jewish law. Most observers say that if Paul had not prevailed, Christianity could never have become a world religion.

To keep this from being merely ancient history, one must realize that the dangers Paul had in mind did not come from anything peculiar to the Jewish law, but from the very nature of law itself. All laws are formulated in specific terms that have presuppositions of time and place and culture. More seriously, in attempting to say specifically, "Do this," and "Avoid that," laws always emphasize some parts of human life while ignoring other large areas.

This seems inevitable. No one could think of all that might happen even in one human lifetime and lay down enough laws to give guidance all day every day. In the face of this fact, most Christians have, with Paul, preferred such summary statements as "The whole law is fulfilled in one word: You shall love your neighbor as yourself" (Galatians 5:14). Paul teaches the gospel way of challenging us to the absolute heights of love and sacrifice rather than of spelling out lists of actions we are bound to do and other lists of specific actions we are bound to avoid.

Still, human community living and human cooperation demand some law, obviously, and Paul in his many letters does not hesitate to lay down directives for the communities he helped found. But his major concern is that Christians not descend to making their religion just a matter of keeping laws. Salvation is through embracing the gospel of cross/resurrection with Christ.

The gospel today tells of a centurion, an officer in the army of occupation which the Romans maintained in the province of Palestine, who dared to approach the Jewish Savior. He won Jesus' attention and help, not because "he loves our nation and he built us our synagogue," but because he was a human being who cried out for help.

Moreover the centurion won Jesus' admiration for the personal faith he displayed. He knew that Jewish practice of the time did not allow a Jew to enter the house of a pagan without being defiled, so he sent word to Jesus not to come: "Lord, I am not worthy to have you come under my roof." He trusted that Jesus could heal just as well by simply saying the word. The man received the favor he asked and Jesus' praise that "not even in Israel have I found such faith."

Tenth Sunday of the Year

Reading 1: 1 Kings 17:17–24

Responsorial: Psalm 30:1, 3, 4–5, 10–11a, 12b

Reading 2: Galatians 1:11–19

Gospel: Luke 7:11–17

one . . . catholic . . . Church

the resurrection of the dead

In today's reading from Galatians Paul continues to defend, for his wavering new converts, the gospel which he originally preached. His point is that they should not wander off to try other schemes of salvation than the one they have already heard and believed and found salvation in for themselves.

He tells them that he personally had pursued righteousness by careful practice of the law in all its details. He knew that way, and had been fully devoted to it—so devoted that he had even persecuted the church of God when he thought Jesus' followers were proposing a different way. Now, however, he saw that the Christian way was not in opposition to the old way, but that it was an important perfection of the old.

Obedience to God in faith in Jesus Christ is the fulfillment of all that the law formerly tried to spell out for us. The one who lives in perfect love does more than any law or set of laws could ever dare demand. But perfect love is not the result of our own efforts. It is God's gift to those who ask it in faith, trusting to the way God has shown us in Christ's death and resurrection. Those who have found God by this way—like those Gentiles to whom Paul had preached—have no need to turn back and try now also to recover, step by step, point by point, the former way of obedience to the old law. If they have given themselves to Christ, if they try to live in perfect love and forgiveness, in generosity and humility, God will give them ample opportunity to prove their faith through good deeds.

The gospel of Christ, preached by Paul, is a gospel of life out of death: "suffered under Pontius Pilate, was crucified, died and was buried. On the third day he rose again, according to the Scriptures." This death/resurrection theme touches every moment of our lives, every life-situation, every day. It covers sickness, weakness, doubt, failure, loss, and fear. Our cross, our little death, may be the loss of someone we loved; or of something we need or think we need. It may be a collapse into sin that has killed us; or some hurt we have unjustly received.

Whatever it is, the good news is that we can and will rise from it in Christ if we face it as Christ did. In its most powerful form, this message is the bold assurance that God will raise up our very bodies from death. As we say in the Creed, "We look for the resurrection of the dead"—all the dead. Any traveler visiting the churches and art galleries of Europe is struck by how often this theme is repeated in great paintings, altar-tables, frescoes, windows. "The resurrection of the dead"—the good to a reward, the evil to judgment—is an image that has possessed the Christian mind throughout the ages. "He will come again . . . to judge the living and the dead."

This idea is illustrated in today's gospel, as in the other gospel stories where people are raised from the dead: Lazarus, the daughter of Jairus. Here it is the only son of a widow. Jesus, without being asked, simply touches the bier and orders the dead man to arise. He came back to life, and Jesus gave him to his mother.

This is taken by the people as a sign that "a great prophet has arisen among us," for the like had never been seen since the days of Elijah the prophet. The story about Elijah is given in the selection from Kings. And of course it is no accident that the stories themselves make clear the great difference between Christ and Elijah. The great prophet of the Old Testament must cry to the Lord, plead with him, stretch himself upon the dead child three times, pray again, until "the Lord hearkened to the voice of Elijah"; Jesus simply speaks the words of healing in his own name: "I say to you, Arise." We are to understand that Jesus is not only "a great prophet": of Jesus it is also true to say, "God has visited his people."

Jesus presented the message of death and resurrection even in his symbolic actions, miracles, and signs, before he preached it in the way that really counts—by going through death and resurrection himself for our sake. He has "all power in heaven and on earth." "Through him all things were made." As is said of his coequal Holy Spirit, he too is "the Lord, the giver of life." He acts "for our salvation." And so we "look for the resurrection of the dead" because he promised it. Meanwhile, if we are trying to live by the gospel, we experience little resurrections from the dead in our lives over and over, day by day.

Eleventh Sunday of the Year

Reading 1: 2 Samuel 12:7–10, 13
Responsorial: Psalm 32:1–2, 5, 7, 11
Reading 2: Galatians 2:16, 19–21
Gospel: Luke 7:36–8:3

the forgiveness of sins

In the powerful story in today's gospel, Simon the Pharisee is scandalized at the excessive liberties taken by the woman of the city who came uninvited to a party in his house. There she was at Jesus' feet, weeping in public, wetting his feet with her tears, wiping them with her hair, kissing his feet, and anointing them with ointment from a precious flask—excessive in every way. The Pharisee, watching it, thinks, "How can Jesus allow this? If he were really a prophet, he would know who and what sort of woman this is who is touching him, and clearly he would not allow it."

But Jesus' answer to Simon's thoughts turns the tables. He points out that the woman's apparently excessive demonstrations are the natural result of her having been forgiven many sins. Of course she is beside herself with gratitude and love. "But you, Simon, you show me no signs of love and gratitude. This clearly implies that you have not been forgiven many sins; you have been forgiven very little."

If Simon remains locked in himself in pharisaic self-satisfaction, he may simply take those words at face value, and say to himself, "Oh yes, that is true. I have never sinned very much, so it is true I have very little that needs forgiveness." However, it is not very likely he could leave it at that. First of all, Jesus clearly takes for granted that one who is forgiven somehow owes *him* love and gratitude. This makes sense only if Jesus is in the place of God, who alone can forgive sins. This would get the Pharisee thinking, either in anger, "Jesus has blasphemed" (cf. Luke 5:21), or perhaps, more seriously, "What if this is true? If this man is indeed in the place of God and can speak for God, and if he then should be treated not only as a prophet but as God himself, then I have much for which to repent; then I have been very wrong; then I do need forgiveness. But he has just told me that I have been forgiven very little. . . ." And that realization might bring Simon to *his* knees with tears in his eyes, falling at Jesus' feet.

David, in the first reading, confessed his sin when the words of the prophet made him realize its enormity; and God forgave him. But we are not told how Simon's story ended, because the important thing is not what a Pharisee named Simon may once have realized, but what we come to realize when we read about him.

We say we believe in "the forgiveness of sins." This implies that we realize how much we have to be forgiven—how imperfect, how harmful our lives are. Often, especially living in a corrupt society, we measure ourselves by those around us and think of ourselves as good people. But what if our whole society is shot through with sin and wickedness, as the New Testament judges the world to be (1 John 2:16)? We can truly judge our own goodness or virtue only by the standard of the perfect love and complete self-sacrifice of Christ. There is no other safe norm of real goodness. We have read Jesus' great sermon. We have meditated on his passion, death, and resurrection. We know the great commandments he has left us. Those are the measure of how much we may need forgiveness, of how wrong our lives have been in the past and perhaps are even now.

Baptism gives us God's forgiveness and starts us on the right path, Christ's path. But the power of baptism needs frequent renewal by life in the church, using the sacraments, listening to the word of God; coming to know Christ better in prayer and faithful service.

We are in a process of transformation; that is our Christian life. As Paul says in Galatians "I have been crucified with Christ; it is no longer I who live, but Christ who lives in me. And the life I now live in the flesh I live by faith in the Son of God, who loved me and gave himself for me." That is the key to the life of forgiveness and love to which today's gospel invites us. We should remember that the Son of God loved us and gave himself for us; live by faith in that great act of his love and forgiveness to us; and let Christ live his life of love, self-sacrifice, and universal forgiveness in us, in our flesh, all our days.

Twelfth Sunday of the Year

Reading 1: Zechariah 12:10–11
Responsorial: Psalm 63:1abc, 1d–3, 4–5, 7–8
Reading 2: Galatians 3:26–29
Gospel: Luke 9:18–24

for us and for our salvation

    The gospel picks up a point made last Sunday as well—Jesus is more than Elijah, more than one of the old prophets. In fact, he is more, greater, than John the Baptist, than whom—Jesus himself said—no greater had been born of woman. Who then is Jesus? He is the "Christ of God."
    It was Peter who saw and confessed that by the inspiration of God. Jesus is the Christ, the Son of God. This gospel then reveals something that people did not know at that time; namely, that the Christ of God was coming not as a glorious redeemer, not as a military or political savior, but in quite another way. To be the Christ of God in fact meant "to suffer many things and be rejected by all and be killed and on the third day be raised."
    Ah, that is a different story! Many might be willing to follow a messiah who had abundant success, riches, and honors to bestow. But this Messiah must die in order to come into his glory. When we say, "We believe in one Lord, Jesus Christ," we repeat the confession of Peter. Immediately we should hear the words Jesus next addressed to all: "If any man would

come after me, let him deny himself and take up his cross daily and follow me." Jesus died and rose for our sake—that we might do the same. "Whoever would save his life will lose it; and whoever loses his life for my sake will find it"; that is, those who believe and follow can expect the resurrection of the body and life everlasting.

In faithful following, we become other Christs. We become, says Paul to the Galatians "sons of God through faith." Our baptism means that this is the only human difference that ultimately matters: whether we have put on Christ or not, chosen his way or not, opened ourselves to live his life or not. If we have, no other difference can be important. Then "there is neither Jew nor Greek, there is neither slave nor free, there is neither male nor female, for you are all one in Christ Jesus"; all children of God, "heirs according to the promise."

Thirteenth Sunday of the Year

Reading 1: 1 Kings 19:16b, 19–21
Responsorial: Psalm 16:1–2a, 5, 7–8, 9–10, 11
Reading 2: Galatians 5:1, 13–18
Gospel: Luke 9:51–62

one holy . . . Church

    Today we concentrate on the holiness of the church, one of the four marks of the church listed in the Creed: "one holy catholic and apostolic." All members of the church, as the church itself, as the body of Christ on earth, are called to perfect holiness. The prayer of today's mass reminds us of that call: "Father, you call your children to walk in the light of Christ. Free us from darkness and keep us in the radiance of your truth." And again in the prayer, "Called to that light, we ask for your guidance. Form our lives in your truth, our hearts in your love."
    Within the church, through prayer and the sacraments, we ourselves become instruments of holiness for spreading Christ's love in the world. So the prayer after communion asks, "Lord, may this sacrifice and communion give us a share in your life and help us bring your love to the world."
    The readings of the mass illustrate our call to holiness in the church. It is a call to follow Jesus to Jerusalem to his cross and resurrection. It is a call to spread his message of love and forgiveness and reconciliation. So, in the gospel, we see that

when Jesus knew that the days were near for him to be delivered, "he set his face to go to Jerusalem." But he wanted followers, so "he sent messengers ahead of him."

Jesus accepted those who said they were willing to follow—but not without making clear what the following would be like, how difficult and all-consuming. "I will follow you wherever you go," said one. "Foxes have holes and birds of the air have nests; but the Son of Man has nowhere to lay his head." Will you still follow? With no sure, fixed place on earth to call your own?

Jesus promises nothing in this world, though he does promise life everlasting. You will get no money, will not acquire property, if you truly follow. In fact, you are likely to find such things only a greater burden for yourself. You will have no fixed abode, because you are not likely to fit too well into human society as it now functions. The world is not designed to operate in accordance with Jesus' principles. Will you still follow?

Think of the peremptoriness of Jesus' demand. He brooks no hesitancy, no opposition, no delay. He lets his service and following take second place to nothing. For instance, in the reading from Kings, Elijah allows his disciple to go home and kiss father and mother. Jesus will not allow taking time to wait for a father's death and funeral. Wait for nothing. Now is the acceptable time; now is the day of salvation.

Elijah allows his disciple to go home and hold a farewell banquet. Jesus says to one who asks to go home to say farewell, "No one who puts his hand to the plow and looks back is fit for the kingdom of God."

Why this strictness, this urgent demand? Because that fits our real-life situation here and now. We must respond to grace when it comes. The moment we appreciate the call of Christ, the meaning of the gospel we have heard all our lives, is the moment to act. If we put up little delays, take time to think it over, say we will get to it tomorrow, it may be too late.

First of all, we may never see tomorrow. Secondly, all the pressures of life are against our complete surrender to the one thing necessary. If we take time, put in little pauses and delays, then we have made our decision *now*. For decision is always now. If we say, "Tomorrow," we have decided *No* for today. Then Jesus is on his way to Jerusalem, and we are left behind. He may not call down fire from heaven upon us, as the more eager of his disciples want to do, but we may have wasted our own lives in that one moment's delay.

Perhaps we were on the verge in that one moment of becoming another Francis of Assisi—who, at the crucial moment of challenge, stripped himself of all he wore, right down to the skin, and walked off to follow God's call.

Perhaps this was for us the deciding moment, comparable to Augustine's hearing the child singing "Take and read." The text to which he then chanced to open his Bible was "not in reveling and drunkenness, not in debauchery and licentiousness . . . but put on the Lord Jesus Christ, and make no provision for the flesh, to gratify its desires" (Romans 13:13f). He knew those words were addressed to him. He could and would live by them. It was his moment of absolute conversion and transformation.

Perhaps in following this moment we would have been like Ignatius Loyola, deciding to forego our pursuit of worldly glory and try instead to do the great deeds of the greatest saints; or like Francis Xavier, being struck by the text, "What does it profit a man if he gain the whole world, and suffer the loss of his own soul?" Who knows what we failed to realize, what resolutions we failed to make, what change of life, what yielding to what new grace we failed to achieve because we hesitated, looked back, delayed one day? and will we be granted another?

The call to holiness is made to the whole church and to each one individually. It is a call that we "through love be servants of one another," as Paul writes the Galatians. It is not a difficult or complicated call, for he adds, "the whole law is fulfilled in one word, 'You shall love your neighbor as yourself.' "

The inspiration to this call and the grace to live according to it are gifts of the Spirit; and Paul tells us to "walk by the Spirit and do not gratify the desires of the flesh." This is the way God's Spirit builds here on earth one catholic and apostolic church which is truly holy.

Fourteenth Sunday of the Year

Reading 1: Isaiah 66:10–14c

Responsorial: Psalm 66:1–3a, 4–5, 6–7a, 16, 20

Reading 2: Galatians 6:14–18

Gospel: Luke 10:1–12, 17–20

one . . . apostolic Church

Today's gospel continues to develop the picture of what we mean by the church; now, as apostolic. We have already seen that being apostolic means the church is founded on the first apostles. But the word also gives us something of the essential nature of the church in all times. That is, it is not a purely factual statement about the age of the church. That the church is apostolic signifies also and especially that it continues the *mission* of the apostles.

So in today's gospel we see the first group sent out to continue the mission of the twelve whom Jesus first chose and sent (Luke 9:1–9). This is the larger group of the "seventy others." The Lord appoints them and sends them ahead of him, two by two, as we saw James and John last week sent ahead of him to a Samaritan village. When that first pair got no response to their preaching, they wanted to destroy the town, but Jesus rebuked them. Here, as he sends out the next seventy disciples, he gives fuller instructions. It is a picture of how the church can be apostolic in every age and have the apostolic success Christ wills for it.

Before all else, laborers are needed. The world is waiting to be harvested for God in Christ. But people must hear the message somehow. That means someone must go and tell them. And each of us must pray to the Lord to keep sending abundant laborers to continue the church's apostolic mission.

How do the church's messengers carry out the mission? Not so much by any great flow of words as by what they do and what they are. They are to go as lambs in the midst of wolves; that is, defenseless as far as the weapons of this world are concerned, and ready to be devoured if necessary. They have no wealth or power of this world, and travel without purse, bag, or sandals. That means they are on the way, not settled in. They have an urgent message, and there are always many other towns ahead. They travel light—without baggage, food, provisions. They travel poor, as the poorest of the poor.

They move with great urgency to their task, for the time is short and pressing. So short it is like the time of the rushed mission which Elisha the prophet gave to his servant Gehazi, to go at once and try to raise to life the son of the widow who had helped him: "Gird up your loins and take my staff in your hand and go. If you meet anyone, do not salute him; and if any one salutes you, do not reply" (2 Kings 4:29). So the church's missionaries, preaching apostles, cannot pause for idle chatter, but push relentlessly on.

When they need lodging, they simply stop, enter a house, and wish the inhabitants peace. If they are received, fine; if not, they go on. If they are received, they live with the people of that house, accepting what hospitality they are given; not searching out better quarters or worse, but just receiving what they are handed so long as they continue their work.

When they enter a town, they make no provision for themselves, worry not about "what shall we eat or what shall we drink or with what shall we be clothed?" (Matthew 6:31), but simply take what is given, if anything. They do their work: healing the sick and telling all the people that the kingdom of God is near.

Finally, the instructions continue, if you are not received, do not worry about that either. Be sure they have heard the message, then leave and forget that place. There are too many others waiting. Jesus adds, in a sentence which is not quoted in our selection today, "Who hears you, hears me; and who rejects you, rejects me; and he who rejects me, rejects him who sent me."

We are called then to do this in all confidence. If we do, we are assured that the powers of hell have no more strength against us. The disciples found that "even the demons are subject to us in your name" and Jesus agreed: "I saw Satan falling like lightning from heaven." With our lives so devoted to his cause, no power of earth can hurt us either: "I have given you authority to tread upon serpents and scorpions, and over all the power of the enemy, and nothing shall hurt you."

These directives and promises remind us of the sending scene at the end of the gospel of Mark:

> Go into all the world and preach the gospel to the whole creation. He who believes and is baptized will be saved; but he who does not believe will be condemned. These signs will accompany those who believe: in my name they will cast out demons; they will speak in new tongues; they will pick up serpents; and if they drink any deadly thing, it will not hurt them. They will lay their hands on the sick; and they will recover." (Cycle B, gospel for the Ascension)

The church is most truly apostolic when its whole concern is on delivering Christ's message. It delivers the message minimally and indispensably by preserving the gospel through the ages, more fully by explaining and applying the gospel well to the needs of each new age, and most effectively of all by living the message. That is what the church is for.

Paul says to the Galatians, "Far be it from me to glory except in the cross of our Lord Jesus Christ. By it the world has been crucified to me, and I to the world." His mind, as the mind of any true apostle, is on one thing only, what he calls "a new creation." He has nothing to fear from the world: "Let no man trouble me; for I bear on my body the marks of Jesus."

An apostolic church must be able to say the same. And the church can say it only if it is true of us, who make up the church. If we are concerned for the new creation in Christ, if we bear on our body the marks of Jesus, and glory only in the cross of our Lord "by which the world has been crucified to me and I to the world," then we have what the world most needs. To be an apostolic church is to bring that to the world continually. When the church is preaching this message, then it speaks most fully with the voice of Christ—and one who rejects it is rejecting Christ himself.

Fifteenth Sunday of the Year

Reading 1: Deuteronomy 30:10–14

Responsorial: Psalm 69:13, 16, 29–30, 32–33, 35ab, 36

Reading 2: Colossians 1:15–20

Gospel: Luke 10:25–37

God from God, Light from Light . . .
Through him all things were made.

Today and for the next three Sundays the second reading is from the letter of Paul to the Colossians. The letter is full of profound dogmatic and moral instruction, and you may want to read the entire text, meditating on it alone, as well as listening to the small selections which will be heard each Sunday.

The beautiful passage chosen for today describes Jesus as "the image of the invisible God." The image of the invisible—the picture of what cannot be seen. As John says, "No one has ever seen God; the only-begotten Son, he has revealed him." When we see Jesus, we do see God. For he is "God from God, Light from Light, true God from true God . . one in being with the Father."

In the Creed we confess, "through him all things were made." Colossians says Christ "is the first-born of all creation, for in him all things were created, in heaven and on earth, visible and invisible, whether thrones or dominions or principalities or authorities." Here the author names some of what later theologians have called the choirs of angels. But he uses names which could apply to any power, government, or force of this earth. The point is that all things that exist were created through Christ and for him.

The whole world centers on Christ, aims at him, is trying to grow to be him. He links God to the world and the world to God. "He is before all things, and in him all things hold together. He is the head of the body, the church." So we in particular move toward God through him. "He is the beginning, the first-born from the dead, that in everything he might be pre-eminent." "In him all the fullness of God was pleased to dwell" that God might dwell with us and be in us. Through Christ "God has been pleased to reconcile to himself all things, making peace by the blood of his cross."

And what does this mean practically? Like the glorious statements in the first part of the Creed, it can seem remote from real life until we read it in the context of the gospel. If Jesus is so important, then what he says and does and teaches is very important to us. And he says, for instance, that the way to eternal life is to observe the one double commandment: "You shall love the Lord your God with all your heart, and with all your soul, and with all your strength, and with all your mind, and your neighbor as yourself."

As the reading from Deuteronomy teaches, there is nothing subtle or really obscure about salvation: "The word is near you; it is in your mouth and in your heart." Paul, commenting on this text in Romans 10, tells what that word really is: "It is the word of faith which we preach; because if you confess with your lips that Jesus is Lord and believe in your heart that God raised him from the dead, you will be saved."

But if you say Jesus is Lord, then you remember Jesus warned, "Why do you say to me, 'Lord, Lord,' and not do what I tell you?" (Luke 6:46). Today he tells us how to love our neighbor as ourselves. We do it not by asking first, Who is my neighbor? (like the immature person asking about each commandment, How far can I go?). We do it simply by first acting like a neighbor to anyone we see in need. To find a neighbor, be a neighbor. To find a neighbor, do not look up definitions first to see who you may be bound to help. Go at it as Christ did: love first and ask questions afterwards. Be ready to help, and you will find neighbors everywhere you look.

Jesus, the original good samaritan, has given his all for us. That is how and why he is the link between heaven and earth of which Colossians speaks. Now we, as his body, his church, are to continue to live up to that one simple word of love of God in our neighbor. "Go and do likewise."

Sixteenth Sunday of the Year

Reading 1: Genesis 18:1–10a

Responsorial: Psalm 15:2–3a, 3bc–4ab, 5

Reading 2: Colossians 1:24–28

Gospel: Luke 10:38–42

one . . . Church

the communion of saints

Today's selection from Colossians speaks of the Christian life as a growing up in Christ: "the mystery, which is Christ in you . . . him we proclaim, teaching every man in all wisdom, that we may present every man mature in Christ." We grow to maturity in Christ. Christ grows and lives in us. This is "the mystery hidden for ages and generations and now manifest." We, as Christ's church, are his living body. This is our "hope of glory."

As members of Christ's body, we are all part of one another, as the various parts of the body all belong to one another. And as one part of the body can help another, so we can help the rest of the body. If we bear sufferings unjustly as Christ did, he lives again in us and is stronger in his whole body on earth.

So in today's passage Paul is saying, "I rejoice in my sufferings for your sake." We can pray and suffer for one another, and can help one another with our sufferings accepted in love. This is part of the doctrine of "the communion of saints." Moreover, "in my flesh I complete what is lacking in Christ's afflictions for the sake of his body, that is the church." So Christ lives again through the ages in us, in his church, the pattern of salvation through suffering, death, and resurrection that he lived in Galilee and Jerusalem centuries ago. If we deny him our bodies, our minds, we are denying Christ the fullness of growth he wants to have through his body, the church.

The lives we choose to live, lives through which the mystical body of Christ will come to its full growth, are various. Any and all of many different works, as we have seen, can be inspired by one same Spirit, distributing to each according to his will. In today's gospel, the church has found the classical types of one major division of vocations called the active and the contemplative lives. Martha consumed herself with much serving, and went to the Lord to complain of her sister, who had left her alone to serve. Her sister, Mary, was sitting at the Lord's feet and listening to his teaching—the classic role of the contemplative, the scholar, the student.

The Lord's reply did not rank active and contemplative life, saying one was better than the other. How could he, if one Spirit calls to both? How could he, for instance, rebuke Martha for serving, when he said, "The greatest among you shall be as he who serves," and "Who is greater? The one who sits at table or the one who serves? But I am among you as he who serves" (Luke 22:26f)?

Rather, his answer is a rebuke to Martha for criticizing her sister. It is wrong of the person in the active life to think that the contemplative life is a waste of time, and to ask the persons engaged in it to give it up and to come help with the serving. It is equally wrong of the contemplative to think that the active life is servile, fit only for lower classes. The rebuke of that error is found elsewhere in the gospels, and made very clear and strong.

Martha had said, "Tell her to help me. She has left me alone to serve." That complaint was the error. Jesus replied, "Martha, Martha, you are anxious and troubled about many things." (Of course, that too is an error, even for the active life; for Jesus clearly taught not to be of anxious mind about food and drink [Luke 12:29], even as he demonstrated in the parable of the rich man and Lazarus the need of attending to the physical needs of others. Martha must remember that one thing is needful—anxiety is never needful.)

Service is admirable and praiseworthy. But so is Mary's contemplative listening. Therefore, in the face of Martha's criticism, Jesus speaks words of praise for Mary: "She has chosen the good portion, which shall not be taken away from her." Persons disposed to the one way of life and to the other must live peaceably together in one church with that caution in mind, remembering Saint Paul's words about the different parts of one body.

Seventeenth Sunday of the Year

Reading 1: Genesis 18:20–32

Responsorial: Psalm 138:1–2a, 2bcd–3, 6–7abc, 7d–8

Reading 2: Colossians 2:12–14

Gospel: Luke 11:1–13

God, the Father

the communion of saints

Today's reading from Colossians reminds us again of the central mystery of our Christian lives: we were buried with Christ in baptism and also raised with Christ in baptism through faith. As a result, we are alive with Christ, our sins are forgiven through his cross.

A consequence of our union with Christ is the fact that God is our Father, just as he is Jesus' own Father. Today's gospel reminds us that we should approach God as Father in our ordinary daily prayers, think of him as Father, and act toward him as Father. So when Jesus' disciples, after watching him pray, asked him one day to teach them too to pray, he taught them the prayer we still say, the "Our Father."

Here, as the gospel of Luke remembers Jesus' teaching, are the words: "Father, hallowed be thy name. Thy kingdom come. Give us each day our daily bread; and forgive us our sins, for we ourselves forgive every one who is indebted to us; and lead us not into temptation" (Luke 11:2–4).

"Father, hallowed be thy name." This opening says, "Father, we bless you and thank you; we want to live in a world ruled by you."

Then Jesus tells us how to ask for material needs: "Give us each day our daily bread." That is what we need—enough to sustain us for one day each day. No more.

Of course we ask for our spiritual needs as well: "Forgive us our sins." That again is something we need many times each day. Then at once we recall, as we always must, that God's forgiveness of our sins is a great and free gift he has given us in Christ; and that it means we should try to live like other Christs. Our basic minimal effort in that direction is to forgive others as we want God to forgive us; so we say, "Forgive us our sins, for we ourselves forgive every one who is indebted to us."

This is a daily exercise of faith, to forgive all our debts, as we read in the great sermon: "If you lend to those from whom you hope to receive, what credit is that to you? Even sinners lend to sinners to receive as much again. Lend, expecting nothing in return" (Luke 6:34f). And he added in that sermon, "Forgive and you will be forgiven; give and it will be given to you" (6:37). He also said, "Give to every one who begs from you; and of him who takes away your goods do not ask them again" (6:30).

Naturally the same doctrine is present in the prayer that he teaches: "Forgive us our sins, for we ourselves also forgive every one who is indebted to us." Does that sound hard? Do we doubt that we can live up to it if put to the test? That provides the final petition: "Lead us not into temptation." That is, please do not put us to the final test if it can be avoided.

If our prayer is after that model, asking for our daily bread and asking for forgiveness, while we too forgive, and asking that we not be led into temptation, or at least not into any temptation greater than we can bear, then all the rest that Jesus promised will be true without measure or limit. Then, "Ask and it will be given you; seek and you will find; knock and it will be opened to you." How else can we expect to receive these virtues if we do not even ask for them? It is the one who asks who receives; it is the one who seeks who is most likely to find; the one who knocks is the one to whom the door is going to be opened. Have we asked, sought, and knocked in our eagerness to begin living according to the gospels?

He encourages us to pray confidently, importunely. A person pounding at the door in the middle of the night will finally make the sleeping householder get up and answer, even if it is only to restore a little peace and quiet. Fathers on earth know how to give good gifts to their children, gifts that will not harm them, but rather nourish and support them. But God is so much more a father than any of us. He is goodness itself. He is the source of every good and perfect gift (James 1:17): "From him all other fatherhood takes its name" (Ephesians 3:14). And so he will supply our wants and "give the Holy Spirit to those who ask him" with all the gifts and graces we may need.

The reading from Genesis shows that Abraham knew how to pray, pressing his point with God again and again until he had what he wanted. He even bargained with God. We read the same sort of thing often in the lives of many of the saints.

Catholics believe in prayer, and believe in praying for one another, but no one denies that prayer is something of a mystery. Still, we do not need to know how prayer works in order to practice it. Jesus does not explain it, and probably no one else can. Of course God knows our needs before we tell him. Jesus taught that too, when he told us about food and drink and clothing, "all the nations of the world seek these things; and your Father knows that you need them. Instead, seek his Kingdom, and these things shall be yours as well" (Luke 12:29–31).

Therefore the prayer he teaches simply mentions the daily bread for each day, leaving the rest to God. And as to the spiritual gifts—God is more ready to give those than we are to receive them: "How much more will the heavenly Father give the Holy Spirit to those who ask him!"

Of course God cannot be changed by prayer. But we can. And God wants us to pray, probably more for our own good than for any other reason. He does not need the information. But he wants us to pray. There is not the slightest doubt about that. And he wants us to ask at least for our daily bread and for forgiveness and to be kept clear of temptation that is too great for us.

"Who asks receives; who seeks finds; who knocks has the door opened." So we believe and practice. For ourselves and for one another.

Eighteenth Sunday of the Year

Reading 1: Ecclesiastes 1:2; 2:21–23

Responsorial: Psalm 95:1–2, 6–7abc, 7d–9

Reading 2: Colossians 3:1–5, 9–11

Gospel: Luke 12:13–21

God, the Father, the Almighty,
maker of heaven and earth

the only Son of God . . .
Through him all things were made.

We look for . . . the life of the world to come.

These passages of the Creed state the basis of the right Christian evaluation of the things of this world. All is from God, under God's control, given to us for our good and to help lead us to him in the new life. The things of this world are to be used for God's service. By using them rightly, we can make his love felt among our fellow creatures. We can foster the beauty and harmony of human living. We can enjoy them with gratitude to their maker. But we must beware of clinging to them as our own.

Today's gospel begins with an incident in which Jesus turns aside a request to help a man claim his share of the family inheritance. Jesus shows he is not interested in such matters, by answering simply, "Who made me a judge or divider over you?" On the contrary, he warns against letting ourselves get too involved in the search for the things of this world, "for a man's life does not consist in the abundance of his possessions."

As he says elsewhere, "Life is more than food and the body more than clothing" (Luke 6:23). Indeed they are. But how easily we are caught up in the opposite impression and a different way of living and of thinking. And how much of our time and energy can be consumed in it. It is not in the safe providing for the future by wealth and property that we truly build a better future; and it is surely not in that way that we live a better present. Jesus' ideal for life is so different.

The parable at the end of the gospel is self-explanatory, but certainly worth our careful personal reflection. The rich man thought he had his future finally guaranteed—and God said, "Fool! This night your soul is required of you; and the things you have prepared, whose will they be?" Read your newspaper today, count the names of those who have died. What was all their striving for? One thing is worth the striving: a life worthy of the kingdom of God.

The reading from Ecclesiastes makes the same point. All this striving is vanity if it is striving for this life and for a future here. In that light, read the passage from Colossians: "If you have been raised with Christ, seek the things that are above where Christ is seated at the right hand of God; set your heart on things that are above, not on things that are on earth."

You have "put off the old nature with its practices, and have put on the new nature, which is being renewed in knowledge after the image of its creator." "Covetousness," Paul says, "is idolatry." It is a refusal to acknowledge the one true God as the maker of all things through his Son. Covetousness is the illusion that we can have our own direct personal relationship to things, as if they could guarantee us our happiness and security; which of course they cannot. Only the one true God can do that.

What we are in this world does not determine our place in the life of the world to come. For that life, Christ is all in all; and having been slave, freeman, Greek, Jew, barbarian, Scythian, makes no difference whatsoever. What matters is our resemblance to Christ.

Nineteenth Sunday of the Year

Reading 1: Wisdom 18:6–9

Responsorial: Psalm 33:1, 12, 18–19, 20, 22

Reading 2: Hebrews 11:1–2, 8–19

Gospel: Luke 12:32–48

He will come again in glory to judge the living and the dead.

We look for . . . the life of the world to come.

We continue today our meditation on the last things, on what we look forward to. Jesus makes it clear in today's gospel: "It is your Father's pleasure to give you the kingdom." Therefore we are to live in hope. There is nothing for us to fear or even to worry about: "Sell your possessions and give alms." As Jesus says elsewhere to the man who had kept all the commandments from his youth, "One thing you still lack. Sell all that you have and distribute to the poor, and you will have treasure in heaven; and come, follow me" (Luke 18:22).

So here, if we do sell our possessions and give everything away in alms to the poor, we gain the kingdom and provide ourselves "with purses that do not grow old, with a treasure in the heavens that does not fail, where no thief approaches and no moth destroys." We have not here a lasting city. Our treasure is where Jesus puts his treasure. And "where your treasure is, there will your heart be also."

How then do we live here? As waiting and watching: "You must be ready; for the Son of Man is coming at an hour you do not expect." We must be watchful servants. If we believe that all we have is really God's, made by him, we use it only as his property. We are the caretakers. He wants us to have enough to live on day by day, and he will give it: "Your Father knows that you need them. Seek his kingdom, and these things shall be yours as well" (Luke 12:31). He also wants us to provide for one another. Each of us is to be "the faithful and wise steward" who provides for all the rest of God's household "their portion of food at the proper time."

But if we try to run the house as if it were our own, if we try to push around other people for our own advantage, rather than do what we can to help them and serve them, if we concentrate instead on ourselves and our own good times, then we will have a sudden and unpleasant surprise: "The master of that servant will come on a day when he does not expect him and at an hour he does not know, and will punish him."

Does this mean Christians should be predicting the end of the world? Precisely not. The one thing clear is that he will come at an hour we do *not* expect—that day and hour are for the Father to know. We can make no predictions.

Does it mean that Christians should be sitting around waiting for the end of the world to happen? Hardly necessary. It will come to us in its own good time—and it will come to each one of us sooner than we think. The moment of death is the end of this world for each of us. It is the moment for the judging of our lives: "That servant who knew his master's will, but did not make ready or act according to his will, shall receive a severe beating;" "Everyone to whom much is given, of him will much be required; and of him to whom men commit much they will demand the more."

But that life will be judged by a standard beyond what we see; life is not just for enjoying ourselves hour by hour but for service, looking forward to his future coming and our life with him—those truths of the faith are objects of faith. And today's selection from Hebrews is a great statement of the meaning of that faith by which we live: "Faith is the assurance of things hoped for, the conviction of things not seen." The future judgment, the life of the world to come—those are things hoped for with assurance; those are things not seen, about which however we have conviction. What is this conviction? Where does it come from? From faith. It is faith. And the whole Bible, Hebrews tells us, is a series of stories about persons of faith who followed God's word, going where they knew not, doing what seemed foolish and impossible—like being ready to sacrifice even an only son, through whom God had promised endless descendants, believing that, if necessary, God could raise the dead; or like believing that God could give a child to a couple in their nineties. And all those people of the Old Testament went to their deaths in faith, not having received what was promised, but "having seen and greeted it from afar, and having acknowledged that they were strangers and exiles on the earth . . . seeking a homeland," desiring a heavenly country, where God "has prepared for them a city."

Is that not our situation? As they went ahead in assurance and conviction, so do we. We too may come to our own deaths without having perceived our reward—but it is still there. He will come again in glory and, if necessary, at the very moment of death you will see him standing at the right hand of the Father, as Stephen did. He promises future rewards and punishments. These are the "last things," of which theologians speak: death, judgment, heaven, hell, purgatory.

Twentieth Sunday of the Year

Reading 1: Jeremiah 38:4–6, 8–10
Responsorial: Psalm 40:1, 2, 3, 17
Reading 2: Hebrews 12:1–4
Gospel: Luke 12:49–53

his kingdom

For the past two weeks we have been following in our gospel selections a long instruction of Jesus reported in Luke 12 and 13. We have read Jesus' judgment on the values of this world and his account of the true life to which we as Christians look forward. Today's gospel speaks of the urgency Jesus felt in promoting his mission and of certain major difficulties that stand in the way.

"I have come to cast fire upon the earth; and would that it were already kindled. I have a baptism to be baptized with; and how I am constrained until it be accomplished." The baptism with which Jesus is to be baptized is his coming suffering and death (cf. Mark 10:37–40). The fire he will cast is that predicted by John: "he will baptize you with the Holy Spirit and with fire" (Luke 3:16). His mission cannot be accomplished, his message cannot be conveyed, in words alone: the great act of love and sacrifice must crown his life.

But more than that: the full accomplishment of his mission requires that many others be baptized with the Holy Spirit and with fire, willingly taking their share in his passion and death.

That touches the lives of believers through the ages, and with that there will be problems.

"Do you think that I have come to give peace on earth? No, I tell you, but rather division." Is not Jesus the prince of peace? Did not the angels announce "Glory to God in the highest, and on earth peace" (Luke 2:14)? Indeed, they did.

But when Jesus said, "Peace I leave with you; my peace I give to you" (John 14:27), he immediately added, "Not as the world gives do I give to you." When he closed his last discourse with the words, "I have said this to you that in me you may have peace" (John 16:33), he immediately added, "in the world you have tribulation." Jesus' peace is for those who believe. But it immediately sets up a division between those who believe and those who do not: "If they persecuted me, they will persecute you" (John 15:20); "If you were of the world, the world would love its own; but because you are not of the world, but I chose you out of the world, therefore the world hates you" (John 15:19).

In that sense, Jesus has not brought peace, but rather division. He has brought the great division between those willing to hear his word and stake their lives on it, and the rest of the world which thinks all this stuff is airy nonsense, dreams, illusions. For instance, "we look for the resurrection of the dead and the life of the world to come." If that is really true, then by the definition of many, we are sick. If the father wants to give to the poor the inheritance on which the son was counting; if the daughter-in-law encourages her husband in generous service, rather than along the course an ambitious mother had planned for her son—there will be trouble. Jesus' own family came to get him shortly after he began preaching, wondering if he were going mad (Mark 3:21, 31ff). How much more other families? Francis of Assisi's father disowned him. Thomas Aquinas's family tried to seduce him into fornication.

Such fierce opposition to the one who embodies God's message is behind the action in today's passage from Jeremiah. The army of the Chaldeans was threatening Jerusalem, and Jeremiah was consistently preaching to the king and people alike that they should not even try to resist this fearsome enemy, but rather simply to surrender. He was arrested once under suspicion of being about to desert to the enemy; then in today's selection we see that those who did not believe him tried to have him put to death: the typical lot of a prophet at the hands of those who cannot understand the message.

In the letter to the Hebrews Jesus is described as the one "who endured from sinners such hostility against himself," and we are exhorted to consider his example, for it will be repeated in the lives of all who try to follow him. Still, even as Jesus looked forward eagerly to casting his fire and accomplishing his baptism, we are urged to "run with perseverance the race that is set before us, looking to Jesus the pioneer and perfecter of our faith." Can we endure as he did? He, "for the joy set before him endured the cross, despising the shame"; but "you have not yet resisted to the point of shedding your blood."

Twenty-First Sunday of the Year

Reading 1: Isaiah 66:18–21

Responsorial: Psalm 117:1, 2

Reading 2: Hebrews 12:5–7, 11–13

Gospel: Luke 13:22–30

He will come again in glory to judge the living and the dead.

Jesus, in today's gospel, does not answer the question whether those who are to be saved are few or many. But he tells each of us all that is important for us personally, that we must "strive to enter by the narrow door; for many will seek to enter and will not be able." That is, when it is too late, many will want to enter and be saved. But the moment of decision, the moment of division, is now.

When our lives come up for judgment, it will not do to plead that we often prayed, "Lord, Lord"; for he says it is not the saying, "Lord, Lord," but doing what he tells us that matters (Luke 6:46). It will not be enough to say, "We ate and drank in your presence, and you taught in our streets." That is the same as saying, "I know the gospel well; I learned my catechism too. I was a frequenter of churches." That is not the dividing line. He says that he will answer, "I do not know where you come from." I do not even care where you come from. The question is what do you do? Are you a worker of iniquity or are you a true disciple of mine?

He tells us moreover that "many indeed will come"; but they will be, as in his lifetime, an unlikely collection of persons, a collection that we might hardly have expected: "They will come from east and west and from north and south, and sit at the table in the kingdom of God." "Some are last who will be first; some are first who will be last." But judgment there will be. And if we do not "strive to enter now by the narrow gate," then there we may weep and gnash our teeth when we see ourselves cast out.

In their historical context, those words of Jesus were almost certainly a warning to his own people not to think they possessed the kingdom without further trying, or that they possessed it to the exclusion of all others. But the words are not written in the gospel for the Jews of Jesus' time nor are they there to teach us history. They are there to cause us to reflect. Our reflections should turn to the people and the groups to whom we might in our heart of hearts feel clearly superior. They are just the ones we may well see marching in before us.

The church is no less catholic because not all persons have joined it. The church is catholic because it announces one true message of salvation to all, and because it is through that one same message that salvation does come even now to all who are saved. All salvation is through Christ, explicitly or implicitly accepted. That is, all salvation is through belief in God saving us through cross and resurrection; all salvation is through loving, giving, forgiving, not judging, in the way that we have seen the pattern of Christ's cross and resurrection to be lived in detail.

That message may come to different people in different ways. Some of the ways may be very imperfect and obscure, but the important thing is whether or not the individual acts upon them according to the amount of grace God gives in each case. The gospels present the message fully and clearly, and the church exists to present the gospel vividly to every culture in every generation, and to embody the gospel message in such a way that all will be drawn to admire, love, and embrace it. But, as Vatican II points out, although the Catholic Church has been endowed with all divinely revealed truth and with all means of grace, her members fail to live by them with all the fervor they should. As a result, the radiance of the Church's face shines less brightly in the eyes of our separated brethren and of the world at large, and the growth of God's kingdom is retarded. (*Ecumenism* 4)

The letter to the Hebrews encourages us to persevere at any cost in this great project we have begun: "Lift your drooping hands and strengthen your weak knees." If the way seems hard, remember "God is treating you as sons; for what son is there whom his father does not discipline?" "The Lord disciplines him whom he loves."

Twenty-Second Sunday of the Year

Reading 1: Sirach 3:17–18, 20, 28–29

Responsorial: Psalm 68:3–4ac, 5–6ab, 9–10

Reading 2: Hebrews 12:18–19, 22–24a

Gospel: Luke 14:1, 7–14

*the resurrection of the dead
and the life of the world to come*

Jesus' words in today's gospel give two moral consequences of faith in the cross and resurrection. First, "everyone who exalts himself will be humbled and he who humbles himself will be exalted." This is just an application of what we believe about Jesus, who "emptied himself, becoming obedient unto death, even the death of the cross; for which cause God has exalted him and given him a name which is above every name, so that at the name of Jesus every knee should bend" (Philipians 2:7–10).

The other application of salvation through Christ crucified and risen is in Jesus' directions for holding a dinner party. They are very special directions: "When you give a dinner or a banquet, do not invite your friends" Oh? What will my friends think of that? He does not say; he does not care. He just says, do not invite them. Who then? My relatives and their families? No, "do not invite . . . your brothers or your kinsmen." How about my neighbors? Perhaps, but only selectively: "Do not invite your rich neighbors." Why not? What is wrong with all these people? One thing: with your friends, relatives, or rich neighbors, there is a danger "lest they also invite you in return." Oh, yes. That would be terrible. To invite someone who might invite me in return some day! ". . . And you be repaid." Here again, as often, where there is a chance of repayment, one leaves the distinctively Christian sphere of action. Pagans and unbelievers would not hesitate to invite those from whom there was a chance for return and repayment. But Jesus' directions for holding a party do not allow invitations to one of that sort: "But when you give a feast, invite the poor." Ah, but I don't know any poor. Perhaps it's time you met some. "Invite the maimed, the lame and the blind"—to a party? To a dance? "Then you will be blessed." Why will this make me truly happy? "Because they cannot repay you." So these directions are a direct application of our faith in Jesus' way of salvation. By reason alone they make no sense at all. But if you believe that the way to resurrection, life, and glory is over the hill of Calvary, they make perfect sense. Then you too are willing to empty yourself as Jesus did, as we read two weeks ago in Hebrews: "who for the joy set before him endured the cross, despising the shame, and is seated at the right hand of the throne of God."

The only reward Jesus promises is that "you will be repaid at the resurrection of the just." If you put everything you have into helping those who cannot repay you, you will be repaid by one alone who sees all, who loves the world he made, including the poor, the maimed, the lame, and the blind.

But this requires great faith in the fact that there will be a resurrection of the just; great insight into the reality of the world that is not seen. As the reading from Hebrews says, we must live in this world as persons who have come

> to the city of the living God, the heavenly Jerusalem, and to innumerable angels in festal gathering, and to the assembly of the first-born who are enrolled in heaven, and to a judge who is God of all, and to the spirits of just men made perfect.

That is, we must have such faith that we can live in the invisible world. The world to come must be for us as real as this one; more real, because it will provide the norm of our judgments and values and decisions.

Twenty-Third Sunday of the Year

Reading 1: Wisdom 9:13–18

Resonsorial: Psalm 90:3–4, 5–6, 12–13, 14, 17

Reading 2: Philemon 9b–10, 12–17

Gospel: Luke 14:25–33

We believe . . . for our salvation

   The second reading today is the one time we read the letter of Paul to Philemon, so we had better take advantage of the opportunity. The reason this letter passes by so quickly is that it is such a short letter—just a note, barely a page in length. Paul sent it to a friend by the hand of a runaway slave who, before running away, had belonged to that friend. The slave, named Onesimus, got to know Paul in the meantime and became a Christian. Paul was at that time in prison, or at least under custody. That is what he means when he says, "whose father I have become in my imprisonment."
   The letter asks Philemon to take back this slave, instead of punishing him as runaways were typically punished, "as a beloved brother both in the flesh and in the Lord." How it worked out finally, we do not know. Paul said, "Receive him as you would receive me." For him, the slave was his own equal within the communion of saints. At the same time, nothing indicates that Paul was thinking in terms of the abolition of

slavery, which was a social reality at that time. Paul clearly hints that he would like Onesimus to stay with him as his personal servant, but he feels that this would require the permission of Onesimus's owner, so he sends the slave back with this note, and hopes to see him again soon if Philemon's goodness does manifest itself "of your own free will."

The Christian message here proves itself to be not a plan for creating new social orders, but a leaven at work in the society which exists. Philemon and Onesimus will obviously have a totally different relationship after this incident and this letter, even if Philemon should not return his slave to Paul and should not release him. Romans did not normally consider their slaves their "beloved brothers" or receive back runaway slaves with the respect and love they might show a spiritual master and teacher. Where they began to do so, slavery could not long continue.

The reading from Luke's gospel reminds us how absolute is the decision we have made in becoming Christians. It shows once again how uncompromising are the demands of the faith we profess. Do we believe, as we say in the Creed? Then we have chosen the way of the cross. Then "whoever does not bear his own cross and come after me, cannot be my disciple." If we do not want to go this way, we do not believe in the salvation Christ brought us.

As a matter of fact, in the strongest statement ever, Jesus here teaches, "Whoever of you does not renounce all that he has cannot be my disciple." He lays this absolute demand before us right at the beginning, and says we should think about it before we call ourselves Christian, just as before starting to build one sits down and decides whether one has enough money to complete the project, and just as before going to war one ponders whether one has the strength and resources to battle successfully. We think through all the implications before we say, "We believe in one Lord, Jesus Christ . . . for us and for our salvation he came down from heaven . . . was crucified under Pontius Pilate, suffered, died and was buried. On the third day he rose again in fulfillment of the Scriptures."

If that is the faith to which we wish to subscribe, then we

must face the fact that it will demand we renounce everything for its sake: "Whoever of you does not renounce all that he has, cannot be my disciple." And besides carrying our cross, renouncing all possessions, we must be ready for the complete surrender of all attachments to persons and to ourselves: "If any one comes to me and does not hate his father and mother and wife and children and brothers and sisters . . . he cannot be my disciple." Hate them? Yes, in the same way we must hate our own life also. Obviously this is not a matter of bearing personal animosity toward those nearest and dearest to us nor to our own lives; but it is a matter of turning away from them in order to follow Jesus. We must not let our natural love and concern for them be our excuse for not living a Christian life or following God's call to generosity, service, heroism.

He who said, "Love your enemies; do good to them that hate you," is certainly not telling us to hate our family. Yet the family may not think much of a love which would be ready to sacrifice them and their apparent best interests in this world in order to give everything to the poor, the crippled, the lame, and the blind. Clearly discipleship is no light matter. You cannot simply be born into it. You cannot simply take it for granted. Baptism does not end the matter, but only begins it.

Yet how could it be otherwise? We are playing for eternal stakes. We are speaking of a relationship with God the Father almighty, maker of heaven and earth. We are talking about a Son of God who cared enough to become one of us and die on the cross for our sake. This religion business is either everything or nothing. It is not a pastime for an idle hour, not a sweet decoration on the kind of life any reasonable person would have chosen to live anyway. Religion is standing before the living God. It is challenge, demand, looking at things through God's eyes, and finding that the way things really are is quite different from what the world wants us to think.

We have one life in which to do good, to love, to help, to be like God. Establishing roots, acquiring possessions, building a reputation can be such preoccupations, distractions, and excuses as to keep us from really living that life. To see clearly where we are going, we must step aside from them, at least in desire; and perhaps even in actual fact.

Twenty-third Sunday : 163

The selection from Wisdom seems to expect that we will find God's true teaching difficult to understand and believe. It admits that the "counsel of God" is very different from "the reasoning of mortals." It teaches that we "were taught what pleases thee" but can grasp it only to the extent that "thou has given wisdom and sent thy holy Spirit from on high." We have the teachings in the gospel. We may still need considerable help from the Holy Spirit before we appreciate them enough to be "saved by wisdom."

Twenty-Fourth Sunday of the Year

Reading 1: Exodus 32:7–11, 13–14

Responsorial: Psalm 51:1–2, 10–11, 15, 17

Reading 2: 1 Timothy 1:12–17

Gospel: Luke 15:1–32

the forgiveness of sins

The texts of today's liturgy focus on the forgiveness of sins, and we are reminded that "the forgiveness of sins" is an article of our belief, mentioned in every recitation of the Creed. The selection from Exodus portrays how "the Lord repented of the evil which he thought to do to his people." The people provoked God greatly and repeatedly during their wanderings in the desert. God is described as extremely angry: "let me alone that my wrath may burn hot against them." But when Moses reminds him of his promises to the fathers, God forgives the people once again for the sake of those promises. In the New Testament, God's promises are even more powerfully expressed and sealed with the blood of Christ: "This cup is the new covenant in my blood" (Luke 22:20).

In the reading from the first letter to Timothy Paul is giving thanks over the Lord's "appointing me to his service, though I formerly blasphemed and persecuted and insulted him." He says God forgave him: "I received mercy," even though "I am the foremost of sinners." He argues that if he was forgiven, anyone can be forgiven: "I received mercy for this reason, that in me, as the foremost, Jesus Christ might display his perfect patience for an example to those who were to believe in him."

The psalm prays for forgiveness: "Have mercy . . . wash me . . . cleanse me . . create in me a clean heart." The psalm refrain is borrowed from the gospel: "I will rise and go to my Father."

The gospel is the entire fifteenth chapter of Luke. In it Jesus gives three responses to the grumbling of the scribes and Pharisees over the fact that Jesus receives sinners and eats with them. In three stories, he reminds them of how normal it is for anyone to rejoice over the recovery of something that has been lost: the shepherd rejoices over finding the lost sheep, the woman is glad to find the lost coin. In each case he draws the point: must not God rejoice over recovering a sinner who repents?

In the third story he makes his point directly against the scribes and Pharisees. There he tells of a wandering son, one who deliberately wandered away and proved himself in many ways a bad and faithless son. Jesus portrays the natural joy of the father to whom that son finally returns. It is a beautiful story of God's readiness to forgive us.

But it is much more than that. For, in answer to the complaints of the Pharisees that Jesus spent too much time with sinners, he suggests that they suppose there was an elder son in that same family, and that the elder son was not particularly glad that the prodigal had returned. In fact, he resented the joyful attention that was paid his youngest brother. He brooded over how unfair it was to him after his own years of loyal service. He felt no joy over the recovery of what had been lost. Can we not feel how unnatural that would be? But that is exactly the position of the scribes and Pharisees criticizing Jesus' happy familiarity with sinners.

The lesson of course is for us as well. Their mistake, and also possibly our mistake, was to think they had done nothing wrong themselves. Actually we are all forgiven sinners. In light of the life sketched in the gospels, it is clear that ours are selfish, small lives. We do not ordinarily act as if we really believe all our Creed proposes.

Still, God forgives us. But he expects us to be grateful for forgiveness and happy to see it extended to others, as well as ourselves. Therefore he has us remind ourselves of this when we pray, "Forgive us our sins, for we ourselves forgive every one who is indebted to us." Because of this, he has us add, "And lead us not into temptation" (Luke 11:2–4).

Twenty-Fifth Sunday of the Year

Reading 1: Amos 8:4–7

Responsorial: Psalm 113:1–2, 4–6, 7–8

Reading 2: 1 Timothy 2:1–8

Gospel: Luke 16:1–13

maker of heaven and earth,
of all that is seen and unseen

through him all things were made

for us and for our salvation

The reading from 1 Timothy urges prayer for all, for "God desires all men to be saved and to come to the knowledge of the truth." That is a very important part of our faith: the realization that God wishes all human beings to be saved. God is not waiting for us to come to him; he has made the first move. He created us for happiness—and when we try by our sins to frustrate the creation he made and loves, he still offers salvation through Christ, a salvation that takes sin into account, and that therefore lays so much stress on forgiveness.

"For there is one God." The first step in salvation is to come to know that. This is the first "knowledge of the truth" we need: that "there is one God and there is one mediator between God and men." That is, in Christ, God makes clear his plan for salvation through forgiveness, love, self-sacrifice—there is no other. Nor is there a more perfect expression of what that plan involves than the life of Christ. Nor is there a more perfect image of what God himself is like than Christ himself. Thus "there is one God and there is one mediator between God and men, the man Christ Jesus."

Many do not know Christ; many approach God through other mediators, under other names. But Paul says these are imperfect; in Christ we have something better to offer them. Not that they cannot be saved through the means they have at hand. God wants them to be saved, so he will make it possible. But the ways they have at hand are efficacious to the extent that they resemble the perfect figure, the one perfect mediator, Jesus Christ.

Even in Christianity, there is room for other secondary mediators. For instance, Paul here asks us to pray for others. Insofar as we pray for others and God answers our prayers, we too are mediators. But our mediation draws all its efficacy from Christ. In that sense he is the one, the only one. This is also what we believe about Christians asking the prayers of the saints, especially the blessed Virgin. The saints pray for us as secondary mediators, but all the efficacy of their prayers depends on Christ. He is the one indispensable link between God and us.

The gospel of today strikes many as mysterious. It is really only a reemphasizing of a point with which we are familiar: we are God's stewards. He is the creator of heaven and earth. All that exists is his. We use the goods of this world only in his name, and only as his stewards. We will need to give him an account of them all some day.

So it is in the parable. The steward managed all the property of his lord, lived on the estates, kept all the accounts, handled all the money. If the harvest was good, the workers happy, business transactions succesful, he enjoyed the benefits as much as the actual owner of the property.

In the story, when the steward is fired for not having done well, and tells the master's debtors to change their bills, he is really saying, "Pay me less." In letting them out of some of what they owe the master, he is letting them out of what they would have to pay to himself as steward. What they owe him and what they owe the master are the same thing—that is the nature of stewardship. But the steward, being generous with the master's property, wins friends for himself. And so can we.

We are God's stewards. Everything we own is really his. If we are generous and forgiving, it is not our property we are giving away—it is God's. But by generosity and forgiveness, we can win friends for eternity: that is, we can be real Christians, with our treasure where only God can see. Heaven will become our true home.

Well, here we sit, with some money in our pockets and at least a few clothes on our back. Whose? God's. Do we hope to come into heavenly mansions? Then we must put to good use this little that has been entrusted to us. Use it as God would want it used, not as we think it will profit us. For "you cannot serve two masters; you cannot serve God and mammon."

Twenty-Sixth Sunday of the Year

Reading 1: Amos 6:1a, 4–7

Responsorial: Psalm 146:6c–7, 8–9a, 9bc–10

Reading 2: 1 Timothy 6:11–16

Gospel: Luke 16:19–31

We believe . . . on the third day he rose again

maker of . . all

    Today's selection from 1 Timothy urges us to "take hold of the eternal life to which you were called when you made the good confession in the presence of many witnesses." Making "the good confession in the presence of many witnesses" refers to a part of the community's ceremony of baptism. The good confession was the first recitation of the Creed as a Christian, as today, when we renew the baptismal promises at Easter, we are asked, "Do you believe in God . . ." on through the various articles of the Creed; we respond to each, "I do believe."

    So did the first Christians then make this testimonial of their faith or, as they called it, their confession. Paul is telling Timothy to "fight the good fight of the faith; take hold of the eternal life to which you were called then." Formerly when the persons to be baptized approached the door of the church or the baptismal font, the priest met them with the question, "What do you ask of the church of God?" They answered, "The faith." "What does the faith give you?" "Eternal life." Every Christian—like Timothy, like ourselves—has to be exhorted from time to time to reach out and grasp that eternal life which is offered to all who can sincerely recite the Creed.

Then Paul refers to Christ Jesus "who in his testimony before Pontius Pilate made the good confession." Did Jesus recite the Creed? Well, in essentials, yes: "You say that I am a king; for this was I born, and for this I have come into the world, to bear witness to the truth" (John 18:37).

Paul himself, "in the presence of God who gives life to all things and of Christ Jesus," charges his readers "to keep the commandment unstained and free from reproach until the appearing of our Lord Jesus Christ." That is, he looks for Christ to come again, and knows that when he comes it will be to "judge the living and the dead."

The gospel for today is the story of the rich man who died, was buried, and was in torment in Hades. During his life a poor man had lain at his gates, hungry, and the rich man never noticed. While he received good things in life, feasted sumptuously every day, was clothed in purple and fine linen, others were in want of basic necessities. So he went to hell.

The rich man asks that Lazarus may at least go and warn his five rich brothers, lest they too make the same mistake, enjoy the good things they have while others suffer want, and so themselves end up in hell. But his request is refused, for as Abraham says, "Your brothers have Moses and the prophets: let them hear them." That is, it is clear enough in the Old Testament that we have a duty to share with those who have less than we. For instance the prophet Amos says,

> Woe to those who are at ease, who lie upon beds of ivory and stretch themselves upon their couches, and eat lambs from the flock and calves from the midst of the stall; who sing idle songs to the sound of the harp . . . who drink wine in bowls and anoint themselves with the finest oils, but are not grieved over the ruin of Joseph!"

The rich man says, "No, but if someone goes to them from the dead, they will repent." One would think so. Would not someone returning from the dead and telling them their danger make a great impression? But Abraham answers, "If they do not hear Moses and the prophets, neither will they be convinced if some one should rise from the dead." Was he right? Well, after all, it happened, did it not? Someone did rise from the dead—and that someone, Jesus, risen, told us all exactly what the rich man wants Lazarus to tell his brothers. Jesus told us, "Woe to you who are rich, for you have received your consolation; woe to you who are full now, for you shall hunger; woe to you who laugh now, for you shall mourn and weep" (Luke 6:24f). Jesus said, "Blessed are you poor, for yours is the kingdom of God; blessed are you who hunger now, for you shall be satisifed; blessed are you who weep now, for you shall laugh" (Luke 6:20f).

Jesus told us to be "merciful as your heavenly Father is merciful" (Luke 6:36) and that "the measure you give will be the measure you get back" (Luke 6:38). Therefore, "sell your possessions and give alms" (Luke 12:33), and "when you give a dinner or a banquet, do not invite your friends or your brothers or your kinsmen or your rich neighbors" but rather "the poor, the maimed, the lame, the blind"—all those who "cannot repay you" (Luke 14:12–14).

Jesus returned from the dead, and the world still does not believe this. He might just as well have stayed dead for all he is likely ever to change the world's opinion. The world thinks, "I have it, I made it, I earned it, it's mine." Jesus says, "God created the goods of this world for the people of this world. They all belong to God, and God wants his children fed, alive, well, happy. You have no right to use more than you need. You owe the rest to those who have less than you."

If he says to us at the judgment, "I was hungry and you gave me no food, I was thirsty and you gave me no drink, I was a stranger and you did not welcome me, naked and you did not clothe me, sick and in prison and you did not visit me," what will we answer? "Lord, when did we see you hungry or thirsty or a stranger or naked or sick or in prison and did not minister to you?" If so, he has already given us his opinion of that answer: "As you did it not to one of the least of these, you did it not to me" (Matthew 25:42–46).

Twenty-Seventh Sunday of the Year

Reading 1: Habakkuk 1:2–3, 2:2–4

Responsorial: Psalm 95:1–2, 6–7abc, 7d–9

Reading 2: 2 Timothy 1:6–8, 13–14

Gospel: Luke 17:5–10

We believe

Church

"The righteous shall live by his faith," says the prophet Habakkuk in the last line of today's Old Testament selection. "He whose soul is not upright in him shall fail, but the righteous shall live by his faith." The prophet is promising in God's name that all will be well with those who trust in the Lord. He is answering the cry which we read in the first half of the passage: "O Lord, how long shall I cry for help and thou wilt not hear? Or cry to thee violence and thou wilt not save? Why dost thou make me see wrongs and look upon trouble?" The answer is, as usual, Do not give up: "The vision awaits its time; it hastens to the end, it will not lie. If it seems slow, wait for it. It will surely come, it will not delay."

So we ourselves "look for the resurrection of the dead and the life of the world to come." We await the Lord's return in glory when his kingdom shall have no end. But sometimes we get tired, worried; we cry out in fear. The answer is, Sinners should worry. They have something about which to worry. But the righteous shall go on living by faith.

Saint Paul quotes this text of Habakkuk in Romans 1:17, and it was one of the texts that most moved Martin Luther to challenge the spirituality of his day. Luther felt the Christianity in his day was mainly a matter of observing the law, doing what was commanded, and then, if possible, something extra besides. We recognize that as a very superficial and even childish view of religion. Luther claimed it was taught and widely believed. But Luther came to realize that the Bible teaches something different; namely, that religion is mainly a matter of persevering in one's efforts in spite of doubts, a matter of trusting God to keep his promises to those who try to love and serve him. Your actual record of loving and serving need not be the best in the world, for God is ready to forgive. But you must continue to reach out for God, cry out for God, and continue to believe in his word.

The gospel today is also on the theme of faith. In it the disciples say to Jesus, "Increase our faith." The selection we are reading does not include the reason why they asked. But the reason is in the preceding verse. Jesus had just said that if your brother sin against you, you should forgive him: "And if he sin against you and turns to you seven times saying, I repent, you must forgive him" (Luke 17:3f).

That is asking an awful lot, you must admit. Of what example shall we think? Someone calling you a liar? Someone laughing at you? Someone sponging off you? Even robbing you? So you forgive him at 9:00 A.M., and at 10:00 he is back and does it again. And again at 12:00. And at 1:00, and so forth, seven times in one day.

Those were Jesus' words just before this passage, and the apostles' answer, reasonably enough, was, "Increase our faith." That is, we surely do not have enough faith to even think about living by that principle now; please increase our faith. Jesus's answer is not very encouraging. He really answers that they have no faith at all. I wonder what he would answer to us. As he says in a subsequent passage, "When the Son of Man comes, will he find faith on earth?" (Luke 18:8).

Jesus agrees with the apostles that they need an increase of faith, indeed that they need faith, period. For "if you had faith as a grain of mustard seed," he says, "you could say to this tree, 'Be rooted up and planted in the sea,' and it would obey you." Faith can move mountains, faith can move trees. But they can do nothing, because they have not even a mustard seed's weight of faith. And we? No wonder he teaches us to say, "We are unworthy servants."

The second reading, from the second letter to Timothy, gives some of Paul's instructions to a minister of the gospel whom Paul himself had assigned to his duties by the laying on of hands, the gesture we still use for the commissioning of the sacrament of orders: "I remind you to rekindle the gift of God that is in you through the laying on of my hands." This gift which Timothy has received is the Holy Spirit for the work of the ministry, as Paul says, "God did not give us a spirit of timidity, but a spirit of power and love and self-control." And he says, "guard the truth that has been entrusted to you by the Holy Spirit who dwells within us."

Timothy is instructed by Paul in the qualifications of bishops and deacons; he is a link between Paul and the later fully developed hierarchy. The ministry of an officer of the church is performed in the Holy Spirit, who is as the soul of the church. Timothy is instructed in the basic duty of every preacher of the gospel, to take his share of suffering for the gospel in the power of God, and to cling to the pattern of the sound words which he has heard, guarding the truth with which he has been entrusted, in the power of the Spirit.

Twenty-Eighth Sunday of the Year

Reading 1: 2 Kings 5:14–17

Responsorial: Psalm 98:1, 2–3ab, 3cd–4

Reading 2: 2 Timothy 2:8–13

Gospel: Luke 17:11–19

for our salvation

one . . apostolic Church

At the end of today's gospel, Jesus says to the cured Samaritan leper, the only one who returns to give thanks, "Go your way; your faith has made you well." "To make well" is, in Greek, the same word as "to save." The saving, the salvation, of Jesus is a matter of body as well as of soul. The salvation we experience and hope for is a healing of lives in all their aspects, poverty, disease, hunger, loneliness, fear, lovelessness, sin—all the things that can go wrong with a human life. "Jesus saves," proclaim the billboards on the highways, and that is right; he does—from everything, in any time, anywhere.

In today's gospel, ten lepers are healed, but only one returns to give thanks. Jesus says to that one, "Your faith has made you well." What then of the other nine? They too were cured. What made them well? Obviously Christ did. Their cases were as miraculously cured as the tenth's when they obeyed his command. But if their miraculous cure was received without faith, then it made them well only at one level, and that the least important. The whole person needs and wants healing. Bodily illnesses are only the outer shell. They can be healed by God in miracles; they can be healed in other ways. But the healing which counts most is the healing that comes only from faith; that must come from within.

There must be a willingness to dedicate oneself to Jesus' way of salvation, body and soul. It is of this salvation that the second letter to Timothy says, "obtain the salvation which in Christ Jesus goes with eternal glory." The salvation comes only from "Jesus Christ, risen from the dead, descended from David, as preached in my gospel." That salvation comes only as the hymn proclaims it—a hymn which is here quoted, and which was already old at the date this letter was written. It offers a short summary of our faith: "If we have died with him, we shall also live with him; if we endure we shall also reign with him." This is what we believe; and, having once seen it, it is important that we cling to it—for it is the word of God. "If we deny him, he also will deny us," because he must remain true to himself. As Jesus said, "he who denies me before men will be denied before the angels of God" (Luke 12:9); and "whoever is ashamed of me and of my words, of him will the Son of Man be ashamed when he comes in his glory" (Luke 9:26). Again we are reminded that our lives are played for eternal stakes.

The readings of the last several weeks have all been in the form of directions from the aging Paul to a younger person, Timothy, whom Paul had made responsible for certain local churches. In other words, we see here the beginnings of formal church organization. Timothy then is told to "remember Jesus Christ," not for his own sake, but because that is his mission as preacher and teacher. Also, he must understand that as Paul has had to suffer for the gospel, so he must be ready to suffer "for the sake of the elect"—that is, for the sake of the community of the faithful, for that is the task of the deacon or bishop or evangelist, minister, presbyter, or priest.

We believe that the church is apostolic because a line of transmission exists back to the apostles, whereby in every generation a body of ministers has accepted and later passed on formal responsibility for the corporate needs of Christians, especially for preaching and teaching, continuing the message, and for seeing that the sacraments continue to be available to the faithful. It would be a strong confirmation of that truth to read through the entirety of the letters to Timothy and the letter to Titus, even though only parts of them have been included in our Sunday lessons.

Twenty-Ninth Sunday of the Year

Reading 1: Exodus 17:8–13

Responsorial: Psalm 121:1–2, 3–4, 5–6, 7–8

Reading 2: 2 Timothy 3:14–4:2

Gospel: Luke 18:1–8

He will come again in glory

He has spoken through the Prophets

    Today the first and third readings are on the value of perseverance in prayer: "that we ought always to pray and not lose heart." Notice the unusual object of these prayers: the vindication of God's "elect, who cry to him day and night." And Jesus assures his hearers that God will not delay long over them: "he will vindicate them speedily." What is this vindication of the elect? It is the response to their daily prayers: "Thy kingdom come." It is the response to their liturgical prayers of "Maranatha: Come, Lord Jesus" (1 Corinthians 15:22; Revelation 22:20). It is the prayer for the return of the Lord—that "he will come again in glory to judge the living and the dead."

    Luke is writing his gospel at the end of the first century. Many Christians, at least a couple of generations, have lived and died since Jesus left the earth. People are beginning to scoff, saying, "Where is the promise of his coming? For ever since the fathers fell asleep, all things have continued as they were from the beginning of creation" (2 Peter 3). It is for this consummation that fervent Christians prayed then (as now?). Here Luke gives the answer to that objection: Jesus' own assurance that those prayers will be answered soon.

Then he adds the important consideration: "Nevertheless when the Son of Man comes, will he find faith on earth?" That is what matters: not *when* he comes but in what state he finds us when he does come. Luke writes elsewhere that Jesus' return is delayed for a time in order to give all a chance to repent:

> Repent, therefore and turn again, that your sins may be blotted out, that times of refreshing may come from the presence of the Lord, and that he may send the Christ appointed for you, Jesus, whom heaven must receive until the time for establishing all that God spoke by the mouth of his holy prophets from of old. (Acts 3:19–21)

The second letter of Peter explains: "The Lord is not slow about his promise as some count slowness, but is forbearing toward you, not wishing that any should perish, but that all should reach repentance. But the day of the Lord will come like a thief."

When time continued and Jesus did not return, it became more and more clear that God wanted the church to organize itself for the possibility of a long pull, perhaps through centuries. So the letters to Timothy have been, as we noticed, explaining important principles of church order. One of those principles, by which the church always lives, and in which it finds unity and strength, is mentioned in today's selection. It is the Scripture itself.

"From childhood you have been acquainted with the sacred writings." Timothy's mother and grandmother both were Jewish Christians, though his father was a Greek (Acts 16:1). So Timothy has known the sacred writings from childhood. Of course those Scriptures were what we today call the Old Testament—the New Testament writings were still being written, as this very letter attests. For this letter too was destined to become a part of the New Testament canon.

Paul says that the sacred writings—all of them—"are able to instruct you for salvation through faith in Christ Jesus." Even the Old Testament, which speaks explicitly of other things, still can yield a fuller message of Christian salvation if read in Christian faith.

But Paul says that *all* Scripture is inspired by God. We believe that the Holy Spirit "has spoken through the Prophets." That means not that God dictated the Scriptures, for obviously, as we see from this letter itself, human beings wrote the various parts of the Bible, each one for his or her own purpose, but that God always inspired the project. That is, the books of the Bible were written by people filled with the Spirit of God and moved by the Spirit of God; under the Spirit of God they wrote things which God wanted written to be of use to future generations.

The same Holy Spirit who filled the people who wrote this literature also breathes forth from the pages which they wrote. When we read them, that Spirit touches us and inspires us to look on the world as they did, appreciate their values and ideals, their all-consuming love of God.

Moreover, the same Holy Spirit, we believe, inspired the church in the course of the centuries to recognize these books as having been written for a divine purpose. But to recognize Prophets for what they are is a process that can take a long time. No one can do this individually, according to personal taste and apart from the community, as 2 Peter cautions: "No prophecy of scripture is a matter of one's own interpretation, because no prophecy ever came by the impulse of man, but men moved by the Holy Spirit spoke from God." Therefore it is not a matter of private interpretation, but something to be recognized by the church as a whole. That is how it actually has taken place in the history of the church, so that there is general agreement today on the books that make up the Bible.

Our attitude toward Scripture is outlined in the last sentence of the reading: "All scripture inspired by God is profitable for teaching, for reproof, for correction, and for training in righteousness." Therefore, obviously, deep knowledge and familiarity with the Bible is a part of the training of any minister of the gospel, "that the man of God may be complete, equipped for every good work." But it is also extremely important for us all. Marvelous things can happen from the practice of daily Bible reading, just a little, but patiently, faithfully, quietly listening for the word of God, awaiting the inspiration and movement of God, while one is reading. It is one of the finest forms of prayer.

Thirtieth Sunday of the Year

Reading 1: Sirach 35:12c–14, 16–18b

Responsorial: Psalm 34:1–2, 16–17, 18, 22

Reading 2: 2 Timothy 4:6–8, 16–18

Gospel: Luke 18:9–14

one . . . catholic and apostolic Church

    The gospel and the first reading again contain instructions about prayer. They insist on the need of humility when one prays, for "everyone who exalts himself will be humbled; he who humbles himself will be exalted." The gospel text especially is self-explanatory and powerful.

    Let us look at the final selection we are offered from the second letter to Timothy. We have been noticing how in these so-called "pastoral" epistles, the first foundations of the church are being laid. In today's selection Paul clearly considers himself on the point of death. It is probably a martyr's death that he expects, for he speaks of being in prison: "At my first defense no one took my part; all deserted me. May it not be charged against them." Nevertheless, the defense seems to have been successful enough that Paul is not yet condemned, but still looks forward to a chance of a second defense and a second trial: "But the Lord stood by me and gave me strength to proclaim the word fully, that all the Gentiles might hear it. So I was rescued from the lion's mouth." But now he says, "I am already on the point of being sacrificed; the time of my departure has come."

Why? Does he think the Lord will not enable him to make a second successful defense? No, the Lord can do whatever he thinks good. "The Lord will rescue me from every evil and save me for his heavenly kingdom." That is the only rescuing that really matters, and Paul knows he has that assurance. If the Lord also saves him from execution here and now, good, so be it; he is grateful for that too. But he does not think that under Roman law he will have long to wait: "I have finished the race, I have kept the faith. Henceforth there is laid up for me the crown of righteousness." If life has been a race, the goal is near at hand. Paul who once was convinced he would see the second coming of Jesus in his own lifetime now faces the prospect of death calmly, and looks back to what has been important in life. The victor in a race traditionally received a crown. The crown will be given him, he says, by "the Lord, the righteous judge, on that Day"—that is, the last day, the day of the second coming, "and not only to me, but also to all who have loved his appearing."

So the great apostle goes his way, hoping for the resurrection day on which he will receive the reward of his labors. And who will take his place? Well, Timothy, Titus, Barnabas, Junias, all others named as his coworkers and fellow-apostles.

He has left a set of church leaders behind him. He has left a body of writings. He has left a tradition, the words which they heard from his mouth, to which these pastoral letters often refer, and to which he exhorts them to remain loyal at any cost. He has left a pattern of suffering for the gospel, and of bold preaching likely to provoke persecution. Above all, he has left fervent communities, calling on God, who is never deficient in his grace. Those communities know they are one in the Lord, their leaders are in communion with one another and with the other communities around the little Mediterranean world. The church is on its way through history.

Thirty-First Sunday of the Year

Reading 1: Wisdom 11:22–12:2

Responsorial: Psalm 145:1–2, 8–9, 10–11, 13cd–14

Reading 2: 2 Thessalonians 1:11–2:2

Gospel: Luke 19:1–10

for our salvation

He will come again in glory to judge the living and the dead.

The theme of both the first and third readings today is the redemption of sinners. They remind us that God's mercy and forgiveness extend even to those whom the rest of us think are perhaps the worst people of all.

In the gospel, Zachaeus is the example. He was a chief tax collector and rich. Therefore, as tax collector, he was a collaborator with the enemy of the people, the occupying Romans, and he certainly became rich by extortion. That was characteristic of the tax collector in those days, and it made them hated as a class. A tax collector did not just work for a government agency like the I.R.S.; he was really what was called a tax farmer. He contracted with the government to collect taxes. In fact, he bid for the right to collect taxes. The government accepted the best bid for a given district, and the successful bidder won the right to collect as much tax money as he could. The principle was that no one paid the exorbitant amount that the laws really demanded. But the tax collector got as much out of each person as he possibly could; and the government itself got the assured amount of whatever he had bid for the entire district. He personally could keep any difference between the two sums. He was typically very rich.

Jesus today volunteered to go to Zachaeus's house, and everyone's tongue clucked: "He has gone in to be the guest of a man who is a sinner." But the sinner was converted, and that is the point. Everyone knew that Zachaeus was a lost soul because he practiced what was by common agreement an evil profession. And, contrary to Jesus' often stated ideal, he was also rich. Lost he may have been, but Jesus tells us, "the Son of Man came to seek and to save the lost."

Of course Zachaeus's conversion implied some changes in his life-style: "Behold Lord, here and now the half of my goods I give to the poor." That alone is quite impressive, but there is more: "If I have defrauded anyone of anything, I restore it fourfold." Well, perhaps Zachaeus should not have started by giving half of what he had to the poor, because it is very doubtful if the rest of his property would suffice to restore fourfold all he had ever defrauded. In other words, Zachaeus the rich man is not going to be rich much longer. So Jesus says, "Today salvation has come to this house."

As the second reading, we begin today Paul's second letter to the Thessalonians. We will read first Thessalonians next year in the A Cycle of readings. In first Thessalonians, one of his earliest letters, Paul speaks with vivid anticipation of the Lord's return, and in this second letter he implies that many of his readers got excited and disturbed and started doing peculiar things because they took Paul to mean that the great day was just around the corner. He corrects that in our selection today: "Concerning the coming of our Lord Jesus Christ and our assembling to meet him, we beg you, brethren, not to be quickly shaken in mind or excited, either by spirit or by word, or by letter purporting to be from us, to the effect that the day of the Lord has come."

That means we look for Christ's coming again in glory to judge the living and the dead; we look for his kingdom of which there will be no end; we look for the resurrection of the dead and the life of the world to come: but we do it without being quickly shaken in mind or excited. We do not stop living and working, as some in Thessalonika did, so that Paul had to write and command, "If anyone will not work, neither let them eat" (2 Thessalonians 3:10).

Christianity is not a millenarian sect that continually sets new dates for the end of the world and must just as often revise them in order to keep up enthusiasm. The world will reach its consummation when God pleases; and each of us will reach our consummation in the world sooner than we think. On a day we least expect, he will come to us. He wants to find us living lives of effort for the good of others, detached from the goods of this world, but not detached from works of charity, mercy, kindness, and love, "fulfilling every good resolve and work of faith by his power, so that his name may be glorified in you, and you in him, according to the grace of our God and the Lord Jesus Christ."

Thirty-Second Sunday of the Year

Reading 1: 2 Maccabees 7:1–2, 9–14

Responsorial: Psalm 17:1, 5–6, 8, 15

Reading 2: 2 Thessalonians 2:16–3:5

Gospel: Luke 20:27–38

We look for . . . the life of the world to come.

The gospel and the first reading today remind us again of our faith in "the life of the world to come." In Maccabees, the seven brothers and their mother were slowly put to death with horrible mutilations and burning over slow fires, all to force them to break one of God's laws. The law in question was one of the Jewish dietary laws, which only a little over two hundred years later would cause so many arguments in the early Christian church. These martyrs were being ordered to partake of swine's flesh, of pork, and they refused, because the law of Moses clearly forbids it as unclean. As they suffered, they made various retorts to their executioners, and some of these are quoted in today's selection: "You dismiss us from this present life, but the King of the universe will raise us up to an everlasting renewal of life, because we have died for his laws." And, when about to lose tongue and hands, "I got these from heaven, and because of his laws I disdain them, and from him I hope to get them back again." Thus we have here three strong affirmations of belief in the coming resurrection of the dead—and this from a period almost two hundred years before the Christian era.

At the time of Christ, the Jews were divided over the question of the resurrection. One party of the Jews, the most traditional in doctrine, denied any such thing, because resurrection and personal immortality cannot be found in the original five books of the law of Moses. But the group called the Pharisees believed in it, and Jesus agreed with them. So in today's gospel, the Sadducees, who did not believe in resurrection, asked a question about a woman who had had seven husbands in succession, being widowed six times: "In the resurrection, whose wife will she be?"

Jesus' answer insists that the life of the world to come will be completely different from life as we know it here. It follows that the question of whom one will marry in the life of the world to come is a false question, a misunderstanding. That is not a life in which one gets married; it is a life of angels, of sons of God. (He gives no other details as to just what that might mean.)

Jesus does not say that we do not know one another in the world to come. He is not saying husbands and wives may not find one another there. He is saying there is no reason to ask who the wife will belong to, because man and woman will not meet in heaven in order to live again as husband and wife, much less to "belong to" anyone. The idea behind the question is wrong.

In fact, the ideas behind most of our questions about the life of the world to come are bound to be wrong ideas involving misconceptions. We are just as likely to be wrong saying what heaven is not like as in attempting to say what it is like. We just have no information about such matters. You remember the reading from 1 Corinthians from the beginning of this year, just before Lent: "We shall bear the image of the man of heaven." The same chapter (in a passage we did not read) says that our risen body will be as different from the body we laid in the grave as a living plant is from the seed out of which it sprung: "So it is with the resurrection of the dead. What is sown is perishable, what is raised is imperishable. It is sown in dishonor, it is raised in glory. It is sown in weakness, it is raised in power. It is sown a physical body, it is raised a spiritual body" (1 Corinthians 15:42–44). But these words do not really give us much information as to what such a life might be like.

The God who made us out of nothing can make us anew as he will. But what he will do, how we will be, has not been revealed. What has been revealed is bare fact, and that bare fact is all it takes to put an infinite value on our every action. The things we do here determine our eternity. No day is unimportant. The love to which we manage to grow will be our state of expanded being forever. The Christlikeness into which we grow will be the image we bear always. The truth to which we dedicate ourselves and commit ourselves will be our treasure without end. These things last. Money, friends, property, name, do not last. We speak of having them, of possessing them, but in fact they can be actually possessed by us in only a very limited fashion. No matter how much money we have, we cannot really eat much more than three meals a day. No matter how many houses we own, we cannot really live in more than one at a time. No matter how many fleets of planes and cars and ships are ours, we can sit in only one vehicle of one fleet at any given moment. Most of what we call wealth and reputation and power is in the realm of possibility and is highly conditional. It always depends on whether other people will respond the way we think they will—and so often they will not.

Eternity actually seems like some remote and long-term investment when you think of it as a place at which you will eventually arrive. But when we focus on the kind of person we must be to come to "the resurrection of life," then we see that the reality can be ours right this minute; and can stay with us.

It is the experienced possession of Christ and the Holy Spirit; it is the love of God in our hearts, making us generous and forgiving toward all, making us a source and center of love, goodness, and happiness in this world; letting us love God as our Father and rejoice in the gifts with which he showers us day by day. That Spirit is ours, if we will only say yes to it. And no one can ever take it away.

Thirty-Third Sunday of the Year

Reading 1: Malachi 4:1–2a

Responsorial: Psalm 98:5–6, 7–8, 9

Reading 2: 2 Thessalonians 3:7–12

Gospel: Luke 21:5–19

the life of the world to come

Today, just before the end of the church year, the intentions of our readings are again explicitly directed to the last day, the final coming of our Lord. This is the day to which the prophet Malachi looked forward, the day when all evildoers will finally be burnt away like grass, and "for you who fear my name, the sun of righteousness shall rise, with healing in its wings."

Paul's letter to the Thessalonians deals with the problems that arose after the people of Thessalonika first heard the message of the coming return of Christ for judgment. Some of them were so taken by the idea that they withdrew from normal life altogether, "living in idleness, mere busybodies, not doing any work." There was nothing to live for, nothing to work for, if it was all going to come to an end shortly when the Lord returned.

Paul protests strongly: "Such persons we command and exhort in the Lord Jesus Christ to do their work in quietness and to earn their own living"; "If any one will not work, let him not eat." God promises an end to all things, a final judgment, indeed warns us that we have not here a lasting city, that all our works are straw, that our hearts should be in heaven and our treasure where Christ is, seated at the right hand of God. We have studied all these texts this year. But we are not in heaven: We are here. And this world, temporary though it is, is the world God has made. He loves it. He made us to live in it and work in it and in this way and no other to gain our salvation.

He gave us talents, he gave us opportunities, he gives us grace. He puts us in a world where many have needs and we have the talents and the resources to meet some of those needs. The world needs us, needs our love and energy and self-dedication. That is what Christ did in the world. That is what Paul himself did. And this letter points this out, saying the readers ought really not to take his words and draw silly conclusions from them. If they believe his words, then they ought also to imitate his example. He was not idle, nor were the other missionaries with him: "We did not eat anyone's bread without paying, but with toil and labor we worked night and day, that we might not burden any of you. . . . It was not because we have not that right, but to give you in our conduct an example to imitate." Paul could have lived from their support while he preached and taught among them. Jesus had taught that the laborer is worthy of his hire, and so the missionary-evangelist should, when he comes to a place, simply move in and take what they offer (Luke 10:5–8). But Paul wanted to give his hearers examples of how they too should be willing to work, how each one can and should contribute according to one's best ability to the growth of the community in a material way as well as in a spiritual way.

Christian convictions about ultimate values beyond this world in no way imply the uselessness of developing skills, education, work, and trade, if these things are done in a Christian way—that is, as service to one's brothers and sisters, and not for personal aggrandizement. We do not aim at building ourselves a kingdom here. Our kingdom is with God, and its perfection will not come by our building and saving, but by his grace, to which we respond with overflowing love like his and by service to those who need us most.

Today's gospel selection moves our thoughts in the same direction. Jesus points out that the temple, the most splendid structure that his audiences had ever seen, would after all eventually be torn down, so that there remained not one stone upon another. When they asked him when these things were going to happen, he warned them: The end will surely come; but if anyone says, "The time is at hand"—do not believe them. If anyone says, "The Lord is here"—or even, "I am he," do not go after them. Many terrible things will happen before the end comes, but no matter what happens in our own lifetime, it is not a sure sign: "the end will not be at once." We can never know.

But this we can know, and it is what is important: Before the end "they will lay their hands on you and persecute you, delivering you up to the synagogues and prisons, and bringing you before kings and governors for my name's sake." That is, there will be opportunities to bear testimony and to be martyred for witnessing to the truth. That may happen. In fact, to those who are loyal to Christ's teaching, that will happen. He had taught that a household would be divided over his name, two against three and three against two; father against son and son against father, mother-in-law against daughter-in-law and daughter-in-law against mother-in-law (Luke 12:51–53). Here he warns again, "You will be delivered up even by parents and brothers and kinsmen and friends." This we can know, but not when the end is.

But this is our way of preparing for the end—being ready for the hatred of those who cannot understand Christ's way. "You will be hated by all for my name's sake." Is it possible? If we think of the doctrine with which he has entrusted us, it seems clearly possible: Love your enemies; turn the other cheek; forgive everyone everything; give everything away; he who does not renounce all he has cannot be my disciple. . . . What government wants to be challenged by those ideals, or can live contented with citizens who insist on practicing those ideals?

Finally, Jesus makes the great statement of faith again:

"Some of you they will put to death . . . But not a hair of your head will perish." How can both statements be true? The protection God offers does not necessarily save our mortal lives here. Moreover, in the long run, what does saving our mortal life mean? Another ten years? Another forty or fifty at the most? What is that? Jesus lived thirty-three years. Who would not be satisfied to have contributed as much to human development and the world's history as he? What if you are already older than thirty-three and have not yet made any great contribution? Then the proper answer is not to worry about getting a longer life for yourself, but to begin right this minute living in such a way that your life makes some contribution to the betterment of humanity, to the ennobling of the race, even if you live only one more day. Can you not at least lessen the amount of pain in the world—or of fear—or of loneliness—by something you do this very day?

"By your endurance," he says, "you will gain your lives." Obviously not your mortal life, your bodily life, for he has just said, "Some of you they will put to death." But the true life, God's life, given us in Christ by the Holy Spirit within us is gained. In that life we are saved, and not a hair of our head perishes. By our endurance here, we gain that life forever.

Christ the King: Thirty-Fourth, or Last, Sunday of the Year

Reading 1: 2 Samuel 5:1–3

Responsorial: Psalm 122:1–2, 3–4a, 4b–5

Reading 2: Colossians 1:12–20

Gospel: Luke 23:35–43

his kingdom will have no end

The reading from Colossians reminds us again of our faith in Christ's absolute preeminence over all things as Son of God. Everything is under his power, all things came to be because he planned them. As head of all, chief of all, especially of his body the church, Christ indeed deserves the title "king." But in particular he is king of creation because all creation is united to God through him, he having made peace through the blood of his cross.

That is the special twist on kingship which the gospel suggests. The gospel of Luke, which we have been reading all this year, speaks about the kingship of Jesus in the infancy narratives: "The Lord God will give him the throne of David his father, and he will rule in the house of Israel forever." But during the whole long story of the public life of Jesus there is never a word about Jesus as king. Jesus speaks occasionally of the coming kingdom of God, but not of his own rule in the house of David, not that he will be king of the Jews.

That title appears again only at the end, as his death approaches. On Palm Sunday the crowds hail "the King who comes in the name of the Lord" (Luke 19:38), and the elders of the people and the chief priests and scribes bring Jesus to Pilate and tell Pilate that he says "that he himself is Christ, a king." Pilate immediately asks him, "Are you the King of the Jews?" Jesus answered, "You have said so." Then on the cross, that inscription stood over him: "This is the king of the Jews," and those around mocked, "If you are the king of the Jews, save yourself."

Where then is the kingship of Christ? Only on the cross does it become apparent. What sort of kingship is this? John's gospel says his "kingdom is not of this world." It certainly is not. Yet Jesus did conquer the world through his cross. Without the cross, what would he have been in human history? Another preacher, a teacher, a good and holy man: but not outstanding, singular, unique; not the one who "loved me and delivered himself for me" (Galatians 2:20). No one would have written of him, "He laid down his life for us and we ought to lay down our lives for the brethren" (1 John 3:16).

As he says in John's gospel, "If I am lifted up I will draw all things to myself" (John 12:32): this is his glory, into which he was eager to enter. His then is a kingship of love. It is also a kingship of absolute commitment and obedience to God. It is a kingship of self-sacrifice. Jesus' preeminence in these things makes him ruler over all human hearts, and makes it possible for God to open all hearts to him in the Holy Spirit.

Any other kind of kingship is, in comparison with this, false, silly, made of tinsel. Kings of the standard sort have no importance any more. Powers of this world do not last, no matter how great they seem to be in their time. But a kingship of commitment—is that not what was really significant even in the old political kingships, the fact that people were willing to commit themselves to a leader? If the subjects did not obey, if the soldiers did not execute orders, what did it mean for one to be a king? Suddenly the one who had borne that title was nothing, an exile, wandering from country to country, seeking asylum where he might live off his stolen goods for a few miserable years of trembling over the vengeance his former subjects still might take.

But real kingship was always a matter of having people willing to follow you as king. Is Christ a king? Yes, as long as there are committed Christians. We have the chance today to make him more of a king than ever, by sincerely committing ourselves to him, taking seriously his words, following seriously his way of life, as we have seen it sketched in outline this year in the gospel of Luke.

Index to the Articles of the Creed

WE BELIEVE: Holy Thursday; Good Friday; 23 of year; 26 of year; 27 of year.

ONE GOD: 1 of Lent; 2 of Lent; 3 of Lent; Trinity; 17 of year.

FATHER ALMIGHTY: 1 of Lent; 2 of Lent; 3 of Lent.

MAKER OF HEAVEN AND EARTH: 1 of Lent; 2 of Lent; 3 of Lent; 18 of year; 25 of year.

OF ALL THAT IS SEEN AND UNSEEN: 18 of year; 25 of year.

ONE LORD, JESUS CHRIST, THE ONLY SON OF GOD: 3 of Advent; Christmas Day; 8 of year; Trinity.

ETERNALLY BEGOTTEN OF THE FATHER: Christmas Day; 6 of Lent.

GOD FROM GOD, LIGHT FROM LIGHT, TRUE GOD FROM TRUE GOD: Christmas Day; 2 after Christmas; 6 of Lent; 15 of year.

BEGOTTEN NOT MADE: 2 after Christmas; 6 of Lent.

ONE IN BEING WITH THE FATHER: 2 after Christmas; 6 of Lent.

THROUGH HIM ALL THINGS WERE MADE: 15 of year; 18 of year; 25 of year.

FOR US: 4 of Advent; Christmas dawn; Christmas day; 7 of year; 8 of year; 5 of Lent; 6 of Lent; Good Friday; 12 of year.

AND FOR OUR SALVATION: 4 of Advent; Christmas dawn; Christmas day; 7 of year; 8 of year; 5 of Lent; 6 of Lent; Good Friday; 12 of year; 23 of year; 25 of year; 28 of year; 31 of year.

HE CAME DOWN FROM HEAVEN: 4 of Advent; Christmas dawn; Christmas day; 6 of Lent.

Index to the Articles of the Creed : 199

BY THE POWER OF THE HOLY SPIRIT, HE WAS BORN OF THE VIRGIN MARY AND BECAME MAN: 4 of Advent; Christmas midnight; Christmas day; Holy Family; Mother of God; 5 of year; 6 of Lent.

FOR OUR SAKE HE WAS CRUCIFIED UNDER PONTIUS PILATE, HE SUFFERED, DIED AND WAS BURIED: 5 of year; 8 of year; 5 of Lent; 6 of Lent.

ON THE THIRD DAY HE ROSE AGAIN IN FULFILLMENT OF THE SCRIPTURES: 5 of year; 6 of Lent; Easter Vigil and Easter Day; 26 of year.

HE ASCENDED INTO HEAVEN: 6 of Lent; Ascension.

AND IS SEATED AT THE RIGHT HAND OF THE FATHER: 6 of Lent; 3 of Easter; 4 of Easter; Ascension.

HE WILL COME AGAIN IN GLORY TO JUDGE THE LIVING AND THE DEAD: 1 of Advent; 6 of Lent; 7 of Easter; 19 of year; 21 of year; 29 of year; 31 of year.

AND HIS KINGDOM WILL HAVE NO END: 6 of Lent; 3 of Easter; 4 of Easter; 20 of year; 34 of year.

THE HOLY SPIRIT, THE LORD, THE GIVER OF LIFE: Baptism of Lord; 2 of year; Trinity.

WHO PROCEEDS FROM THE FATHER AND THE SON: 3 of year; 4 of year.

WITH THE FATHER AND THE SON HE IS WORSHIPPED AND GLORIFIED: Pentecost; Trinity.

HE HAS SPOKEN THROUGH THE PROPHETS: 2 of Advent; 29 of year.

ONE . . . : Epiphany; 2 of Easter; 3 of Easter; 5 of Easter; 6 of Easter; 9 of year; 13 of year; 16 of year; 30 of year.

HOLY . . . : Epiphany; 3 of Easter; 5 of Easter; 6 of Easter; 13 of year.

CATHOLIC . . . : Epiphany; 5 of Easter; 6 of Easter; 9 of year; 10 of year; 30 of year.

AND APOSTOLIC CHURCH: Epiphany; 2 of Easter; 3 of Easter; 5 of Easter; 6 of Easter; 7 of Easter; 9 of year; 14 of year; 28 of year; 30 of year.

WE ACKNOWLEDGE ONE BAPTISM: Baptism of Lord; 11 of year.

FOR THE FORGIVENESS OF SINS: Baptism of Lord; 4 of Lent; 5 of Lent; 2 of Easter; 11 of year; 24 of year.

WE LOOK FOR THE RESURRECTION OF THE DEAD: 6 of year; 4 of Easter; 5 of Easter; 10 of year; 22 of year.

AND THE LIFE OF THE WORLD TO COME: 6 of year; 5 of Lent; 4 of Easter; 19 of year; 22 of year; 32 of year; 33 of year.

COMMUNION OF SAINTS: 4 of Easter; 5 of Easter; 16 of year; 17 of year.